The Story of Norton, Powys

The Story of Norton, Powys

by

Keith Parker

Logaston Press

LOGASTON PRESS
Little Logaston Woonton Almeley
Herefordshire HR3 6QH
logastonpress.co.uk

First published by Logaston Press 2016
Copyright © Keith Parker 2016

ISBN 978 1 910839 10 2

Typeset by Logaston Press
and printed in Great Britain by
Bell & Bain Ltd, Glasgow

For Joan

CONTENTS

ACKNOWLEDGEMENTS

In writing this book I have incurred many obligations, not least to the historians of the past and present from whom I have gained many insights into the evolution of the village. My thanks are due to the staff of the record offices and libraries visited in the course of my research who dealt with my requests and queries with unfailing courtesy and patience. I am also indebted to Edward Harley who most kindly gave me access to his family's archives at Brampton Bryan, an invaluable source for the history of the Herefordshire/Radnorshire borderland. As far as the more recent history of the village is concerned, I owe a particular debt of gratitude to the contributors to the Women's Institute's *Memories of Norton*.

The closure of the Hereford County Record Office and of the Radnorshire Society's library for much of 2014 and the early months of 2015 presented me with some problems, but fortunately Mrs Jane Banwell kindly gave me access to the papers of her parents, the late John and Esther Roberts, which contained transcripts of several significant documents, in addition to their notes on aspects of Norton's past. I must also thank Meurig Griffiths for kindly translating Dr Llinos Beverley Smith's article, 'Olrhain Anni Goch' into English for me.

My thanks are also due to those who have kindly allowed me to reproduce photographs as illustrations: The Judge's Lodgings (plates 5, 6 and 15); George Lancett (plates 2, 4, 13 and 14); the late Cherry Liversedge (plates 9 and 12); Logaston Press (plate 10); and Joan Parker (plates 1, 3, 7, 8 and 16).

I am also indebted to Andy and Karen Johnson of Logaston Press, who have gently nudged me into providing greater detail and precision in the text and also 'eased' my very formal written style. Lastly and by no means least, I must thank my wife Joan for showing, as ever, considerable patience and forbearance in tolerating my penchant for frequenting record offices far and near and, sometimes at home, my apparent preference for my study and my books rather than her most charming company.

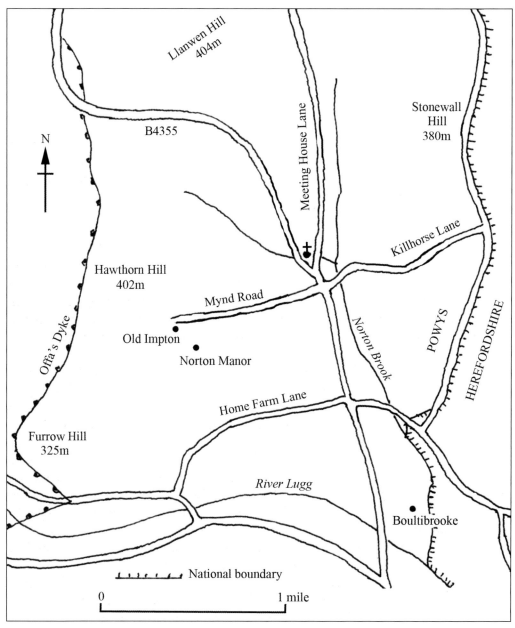

Map 1: The Norton District

INTRODUCTION

The parish of Norton is sandwiched between Offa's Dyke to its west and the border between Wales and England to its east. It occupies the small valley of the Norton Brook and the surrounding uplands, bounded to the west by Furrow Hill and Hawthorn Hill, to the north by Llanwen Hill and to the east by Stonewall Hill, while to the south and south-east it opens out to the Lugg valley.

Norton, or *Nortune* – the North Farm – in the Domesday Book of 1086, is perhaps the most English part of Radnorshire. Its name is Anglo-Saxon while its Welsh version, *Nortyn*, is clearly derived from this, and there appear to be few Welsh place, farm or field names in the parish. The settlement pattern, a single township parish, consisting of a cluster of houses round the church and castle, surrounded by outlying farms is typically English. Again, the local farming pattern, accent and vernacular architecture have much more in common with north-west Herefordshire and south Shropshire than with the Radnorshire heartland.

This is largely the result of physical factors. The Lugg and Teme valleys and the roads run west to east and, until the mid-19th century, links with Wales were made difficult by the Radnor Forest massif. Thus Norton farmers, in common with much of east Radnorshire, viewed Presteigne or Knighton and then, further afield, Ludlow, Leominster and Hereford as their natural markets.

However, Welsh influences in the parish have never been entirely absent for since the late 18th century, if not earlier, the fertile land of east Radnorshire and north-west Herefordshire have attracted successful farmers of the Radnorshire heartland to settle in the locality. Before the Civil War of the mid-17th century, Welsh influences were considerably stronger. Thus at the end of the 13th century probably more than 50% of the population of Norton were Welsh, while in the 16th century and the early 17th century it seems likely that most of the population of the Norton-Presteigne area were bilingual.

Census returns suggest that, prior to the 20th century, Norton was a self-contained community in which most worked on the land, with the routine of the farming year broken only by weekly or fortnightly visits to Presteigne or Knighton market and to the May or Michaelmas fairs in one or other of these towns. Over the course of the 20th century the character of the village has changed fundamentally as a result of changes in agriculture and the decline of its two 'big houses', which sharply reduced employment opportunities in the locality. Today its smaller working population is highly mobile, with most employed outside the locality in Presteigne, Knighton, Llandrindod, Leominster, Ludlow and further afield. With the closure of the primary school in 1958, all local schoolchildren have joined the weekday exodus from the village during term time, heightening the impression that Norton has become little more than a dormitory village.

Paradoxically the population of the village has increased sharply, by more than 70% between 1971 and 1991, with the expansion in housing coming first to the south of the old village. The population increase has stemmed from inward migration, a significant proportion consisting of retired people attracted by the pleasant environment and relatively cheaper housing. In common with Presteigne and Knighton, the age distribution has become heavily skewed towards the over-60 age group, which made up about a third of the population by 1991.

1   MEDIEVAL NORTON

The Domesday Book of 1086 gives a concise description of 11th-century Norton which then lay in the Shropshire Hundred of Leintwardine. It was held, with Knighton, by Hugh the Donkey, a Norman noble, whose soubriquet reflected stubbornness rather than stupidity.

> Hugh also holds Norton. Leofled held it before 1066. 5 hides. Land for 12 ploughs. It was and is waste. A large wood.

Brief as it is, this account gives an insight into the locality at this time. It shows that Norton was a manor of about 600 acres of cultivable land – a hide was about 120 acres of average quality land – surrounded by extensive woodland. Norton had the same amount of cultivable land as its neighbours, Knighton and Humet – the modern Presteigne.

Like them it had suffered severely as a result of the Welsh raids led by Gruffydd ap Llewelyn, particularly that of 1052, from which the area had not recovered some 30 years later. The situation had not been helped by the rebellion of Eadric the Wild of 1068-69 in north Herefordshire and south Shropshire. However the term 'waste' should not be taken literally, rather that the local economy was functioning well below its normal level and its manorial organisation was not yet operating effectively enough to enable a realistic estimation of its potential worth to be made.

Domesday Book also gives an insight into the administrative structure of the Radnorshire-Herefordshire borderland in the second half of the 11th century. During the reign of Edward the Confessor Norton and Knighton, together with 11 Herefordshire manors, had been held by an Anglo-Saxon lady, Leofled. After the Conquest Norton, Knighton and Barland, another manor later to be included in Radnorshire, together with 20 Herefordshire manors, many of them previously held by Leofled, passed into the hands of Hugh the Donkey. Hugh had probably come to England with William fitz Osbern (d.1071), the first post-Conquest earl of Hereford, and served under him defending the English borderland from Welsh attacks.

In its *Historical Survey-Radnorshire*, Clywd Powys Archaeological Trust (hereafter CPAT) sees Norton as a nucleated settlement centred on the castle and church, with the appearance of 'a planned settlement with a regular street layout ... deliberately laid out rather than growing organically and haphazardly'. Certainly the pattern of roads and lanes shown on the tithe survey plan of Norton in 1845 hints at a grid pattern of settlement never fully carried out in practice. Some evidence, admittedly slight, suggests that this Norman settlement may have aspired, unsuccessfully, to borough status. In his *New Towns of the Middle Ages*, Maurice Beresford noted that in the past a separate jury was sworn for Norton, 'a distinction usually reserved for castle towns and boroughs'.[1]

However this Norman settlement was almost certainly not the first in the locality. In the 1950s, three convex scrapers, 15 flakes and spills and a fragment of a polished stone axe were found on fields on Home Farm, evidence of human activity in the locality in the prehistoric period. Again, while not rejecting the possibility of a Celtic settlement in the Norton area, Dorothy Sylvester postulated an 8th-century Mercian settlement, 'a tiny settlement in a limited clearing' in the midst of dense woodland.[2] The 'earthworks of uncertain character' in a field immediately to the south of the Knighton road adjacent to the old school which CPAT identified as the possible site of medieval dwellings may have been that of the original Mercian settlement, though such an attribution is highly tentative. Certainly Norman settlers in a hostile and alien land would have reason to site their castle some distance from such a settlement to reduce the risk of a surprise attack.

The motte and bailey castle stood at the northern end of the village, the site partly destroyed when the Presteigne-Knighton road, the present B4355, was driven through it. The tall conical motte, some 7 metres high, with the ditch around it, lies in the garden of a modern house to the west of the road, while the roughly rectangular bailey lies to the east and stretches from the road to Norton Brook and includes the area now occupied by the old vicarage and its garden along with the church and churchyard.

Paul Remfry suggests that the castle was built some time before 1086 by Hugh the Donkey. Initially it had a timber keep and a palisade around the bailey, but was subsequently largely rebuilt in stone at an unknown date. It clearly had some strategic value in the troubled times of the late 12th century: in 1191 Walter Clifford and Hugh Say were paid for garrisoning the castle on behalf of the Crown and during the next decade or so both William Braose and Hugh Mortimer sought to gain control of it to strengthen their grip on the Middle March. It was largely destroyed by Llewelyn the Great in 1215 and after it had been rebuilt by Ralph Mortimer II at some time after 1230, it was taken by Owain ap Madog on behalf of Llewelyn ap Gruffydd in 1262 and completely destroyed. By the time of Leland (*c.*1540) all that remained was 'a little pilot or turret' and this probably did not remain long. Faced stone was scarce and expensive and the old masonry was no doubt carried off by the locals.[3]

The suggestion of CPAT that the bailey of the castle included the area occupied by the church and churchyard implies that St Andrew's was a Norman foundation and poses some questions as to the place of worship of the pre-Conquest settlement in the locality. One possibility is that the pre-Norman Norton township, like those at Stapleton, Willey, Combe, Rodd, Nash and Little Brampton, was initially part of the *parochia* of a minster church at Presteigne, whose priests served the communities of the upper Lugg valley.[4] Norton's original name, 'North farm or town', certainly suggests some kind of relationship with Presteigne and its *parochia*. The dedication of Norton church, like Presteigne's, to St Andrew, may well be an echo of such a relationship.

Of the fabric of the original church we know little beyond that revealed in the course of the restoration of 1868, which suggests that it was, like most medieval Radnorshire churches, a simple low, stone-built structure consisting of a tower, nave and chancel. Documents of 1397 and 1480 suggest that the parish lacked the resources needed to support a priest itself and was usually held in plurality with Discoed. The 1397 document suggests that Norton was the senior partner in this alliance, for the Discoed parishioners were complaining that the Norton priest had failed to provide a light for the celebration of Mass, or a set of vestments for feast days at Discoed, and also had neglected to repair the leaky roof.[5] The problem stemmed from the fact that Wigmore Abbey, which appointed the priest, had appropriated the great tithes, leaving only the small tithes and glebe to maintain him. Of the priests serving the parish in the medieval period, we know the names of only a few: 1384 Nicholas More; 1466 Geoffrey Claston, appointed on the death of Richard Badlond; February 1467 John Topclieff, appointed vicar; 1467 Thomas Weaver, appointed on the resignation of Topclieff and 1477 John Lippard, appointed on the resignation of Thomas Weaver.[6]

If Norton may have been initially linked with Presteigne ecclesiastically, dynastically it marched with Knighton. On the death of Hugh the Donkey, both lordships were held successively by the Chandos family, then by the Crown, then by Llewelyn the Great. The Mortimers had long had ambitions on the two lordships and in 1230 acquired them when Ralph Mortimer II (d.1246) married Gwladys Ddu, the daughter of Llewelyn who granted Knighton and Norton to the couple as a dowry.

Norton was not always under the direct control of the Mortimers of Wigmore as it sometimes passed to a Mortimer widow to hold for life as her dowry. Thus between 1282 and 1334 Norton was held by two Mortimer widows in succession. Again when the Mortimer heir was a minor, the family estates passed during the minority to the Crown or its nominee. Thus when Roger Mortimer VI died in 1398 his son and heir, Edmund, was aged only six and the family estates passed to the Crown until 1413.[7]

The settlement was wholly agricultural in character with the tenants working strips of arable in the open fields, grazing their livestock on the wastes and uplands of the west, east and north of the parish and working the lord of the manor's private land – the demesne – for a number of days each week as rent. The amount of this customary labour depended upon the amount of land held by the tenant.

In the assessment for a tax known as the Fifteenth – nominally one-fifteenth of the taxpayer's moveable wealth – to be collected in 1293 we are introduced to the 47 Norton taxpayers, some of whom bore local territorial surnames such as de Blackbache, de Bultibroc, de Boresforde and de Stockinge. Four of the Norton taxpayers were assessed as liable to pay 5 shillings or more, 26 between 2 shillings and 4 shillings and 11 pence, and 17 under 2 shillings. The average Norton assessment of 29 pence was significantly lower than the Radnor and Stapleton average of 34 pence, and broadly on a par with Presteigne's average of 31 pence and Knighton's 28 pence.[8]

From the names of the taxpayers, M.A. Faraday suggests that in 1293 the Bleddfa lordship, the poorest of the lordships with an average tax assessment of 17 pence, was 100% Welsh, Knighton 66%, Norton 53%, Radnor 47%, Stapleton 25% and Presteigne 9%. Faraday's view that Norton was one of the lordships with a significant Welsh population is supported by *Calendar Post Mortem iv*, which described Norton as 'in Welshry' in 1304, with the Welsh inhabitants living under Welsh laws and customs.[9]

Living conditions in the British Isles deteriorated sharply in the 14th century as climatic conditions deteriorated markedly from the optimum of *c*.1300, leading to the height above sea level at which cereals could be grown falling by as much as 200 feet by 1350. The Black Death of 1349-50 and the frequent plague epidemics of the second half of the century made matters worse. Climate change and the heavy mortality of the plague epidemics led to labour shortages as a result of which demesne land was leased out because there was not sufficient customary labour available for the lord to work it. In Norton the demesne was leased out in 1334, well before the onset of plague epidemics, which suggests that climate change alone had already led to out-migration from the parish to more favoured areas.[10] The plague epidemics of the second half of the century simply made matters worse.

Another response to climate change and labour shortages was a shift from arable to live-stock farming, with an emphasis on the production of wool and the manufacture of cloth. Norton, like Knighton, seems to have begun to adjust relatively quickly, for fulling mills to cleanse the woven cloth were reported in 1338-39 in both places. The site of the Norton fulling mill is not known, but may have been on the same leet off Norton Brook as that on which the Norton grist mill stood. The latter was in existence by 1335-36.[11]

Norton's adjustment to the new economic environment probably faltered as a result of the devastation it experienced either before the battle of Pilleth on 22 June 1402 or, more likely, in its aftermath. Nor was Norton the only victim, for Knighton was also ravaged, while Bleddfa and Pilleth churches were also destroyed by Glyndwr, who was deliberately targeting Mortimer estates. As Remfry recounts, by 1406 Knighton and Norton were 'so burned and wasted by the rebels that no profit could issue to the king without their better custody'.[12]

By the middle of the 15th century the economy of the Middle March in general and of the Presteigne-Knighton area in particular had largely recovered as a result of the expansion of the Flanders wool trade. The recovery continued in the second half of the century, a contributory factor being the seeming immunity of the area from the plague epidemics which affected the kingdom every decade or so. Significantly, Presteigne, Norton, and Knighton do not figure on Faraday's list of parishes in the Hereford diocese with a high mortality rate in the period 1452-1500.[13]

Norton's direct link with the Mortimers was broken in 1425 with the death of Edmund Mortimer V. His estates passed via his sister Ann Mortimer to her husband, the earl of Cambridge, and then to his son Richard, duke of York. They were thus part of the spoils of the Wars of the Roses fought between the houses of York and Lancaster. On the defeat of the Yorkists in 1459 they passed to Henry VI. Richard of York was killed at the battle of Wakefield in 1460, but after the battle of Mortimer's Cross in 1461, his son, Edward, earl of March, took the throne as Edward IV.

2   Tudor Norton

After the death of the Yorkist Richard III at the battle of Bosworth in 1485 the Mortimer estates in the later Radnorshire, including Norton, passed into the hands of the Lancastrian Henry Tudor, now Henry VII. In 1493 he granted these lands to his son Prince Arthur, but on the latter's death in 1502 the estates reverted to the Crown. The Mortimer estates in the northern and central Radnor uplands had been grouped into the Lordship of Maelienydd since at least the mid-15th century, and for administrative convenience the Mortimer manors of Knighton, Norton and Presteigne were now placed under the jurisdiction of the steward of the Lordship of Maelienydd.

Although economic considerations – the cattle trade, the wool trade and cloth manufacturing – were pulling the Lugg and upper Teme valleys into the English orbit in the 16th and 17th centuries and the parishes of Presteigne, Norton and Knighton lay within the English diocese of Hereford, Welsh influence in the area remained strong.

Socially and politically the area was dominated by the local gentry such as the Prices of Monaughty and Pilleth and the Lewises of Harpton, Welsh in origin and culture and fiercely proud of their princely descent. In Norton itself, the dominant family in the 16th and early 17th century was the Lloyd family of Boultibrooke who claimed descent from Lewis Crugeryr, a member of one of the princely families of Wales, who had held Castle Crugeryr, a mile or so north-west of the A44/A481 junction at Forest Inn.

Impton was the seat of a Welsh family who had gained standing – and wealth – in their capacity as lordship officials. Richard Suggett sees the original stone-built hall at Impton as built *c.*1471 by Rhys ap Dafydd of Weston, who had served as receiver of the lordship of Maelienydd, and extended *c.*1542-43 by his grandson Watkin ap Thomas to provide fitting accommodation for his son Thomas ap Watkin. Thomas had married Elizabeth, the daughter of John Bradshaw, whose family was to dominate Presteigne in the second half of the 16th century.[1] Impton was clearly a house of high status which clearly reflected the wealth and standing of its residents.

The use of the patronymic by the Impton family was by no means anomalous for it was used by a significant minority of taxpayers contributing to the 1544 instalment of the 1543 Subsidy in Norton, Discoed and Presteigne, while as late as 1620 more than 17% of the landholders in Presteigne parish, mainly in the northern and western townships, were using a patronymic rather than a surname.[2] A significant proportion of the population were Welsh in outlook and culture, though bilingual in speech.

Plate 1: Old Impton. (Courtesy Joan Parker)

The New Radnor-Presteigne-Knighton area in the 16th century lay securely within the Welsh cultural sphere. Hugh and Thomas Lewis of Harpton with John Lewis, the son of the latter's second marriage, earned the plaudits of a number of bards, notably Lewys Dwnn and Morgan Elfael. The latter was buried at Presteigne in 1563. As Dr Llinos Beverley Smith demonstrates, Norton featured in bardic poetry. An adulterous affair conducted by the bard Ieuan Dyfi with Anni Goch, the wife of John Lippard alias Goze or Goch of Norton – possibly a kinsman of the priest appointed to Norton in 1477 – gave rise to a love poem to Anni and another, in which Ieuan railed against the wiles of womankind in general.[3]

As Dr Beverley Smith explains, the church authorities reacted vigorously to the scandal for in the course of hearings in the consistory courts of Hereford diocese Anni alleged in 1502 that Ieuan had raped her, while in a hearing in 1517 Lippard alleged that Anni had plotted to poison him and admitted that he had committed bigamy by secretly marrying another woman, while Anni claimed that Lippard had sold her to Ieuan Dyfi. In 1502 the bard was sentenced to be whipped eight times around Presteigne church; in 1517 Lippard was sentenced to six whippings, two each around Presteigne, Norton and Byton churches, while at a later hearing Anni admitted that she had committed adultery with the bard and two other men and was sentenced to be whipped four times around Presteigne church.

Traces of Welsh influence can be detected in the parish as late as the Norton Tithe Survey of 1845 for Welsh elements survived, possibly in the names of two or three farms and certainly in some field names. Bach Farm would seem to be Welsh in origin, though Dorothy Sylvester thinks that it may have been derived from the Old English 'batch' or 'bache', meaning stream, brook or small valley – certainly it was called the Baidge Farm in the mid-17th century.[4] The same explanation may apply in the case of Blackpatch or Blackbach Farm. Again Lysevern Farm in the Tithe Survey is called Llys-y-wern in some other sources.

Farms in the upland areas of the parish certainly had field names with apparently Welsh elements in the 1840s. Thus, on the lands of Hill House Farm there were Lletty Peer, Cwm Birs and Cwm Hanky, while Hares Green Farm had fields named Lower and Upper Wernllwyd. Welsh elements were also found in field names on lower ground in the parish: Wain Waugh on Back Lane Farm and Cross Bwlch on Boultibrooke Farm.

Prominent Norton families
The Lloyd family of Boultibrooke dominated 16th-century Norton by virtue of their descent, the extent of their lands and the important role they played in the governance of the newly formed county of Radnorshire, providing no fewer than seven high sheriffs between 1544 and 1590.

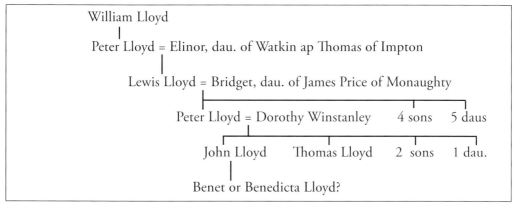

Figure 1: A Lloyd of Boultibrooke genealogy.
(*Sources:* Lewis Dwn, Volume 2, p.254, PCAO, RCB Oliver's draft article on John Read)

The first member of the family to serve in this capacity was Peter Lloyd who served as sheriff in 1544 and 1554. For the second instalment of the 1543 Subsidy the annual value of his land was assessed at £20, the highest valuation of lands or goods in the parish. He married Elinor, the daughter of Watkin ap Thomas of Impton and their son, Lewis Lloyd, served as sheriff in 1566, 1577, 1583 and 1598 and was also, according to E.J.L. Cole, bailiff of Presteigne for most years between 1551 and 1563. He married Bridget, the daughter of James Price of Monaughty, and fathered ten children, while his son, Peter Lloyd of Stocking, was sheriff in 1589 and married Dorothy Winstanley, the stepdaughter of John Bradshaw II.[5] Lewis Lloyd was thus connected to two of the most influential families in the county, but the need to provide suitable portions for all his children placed a huge strain on the family resources.

Thomas ap Watkin was assessed at £18 in terms of the net value of his goods, the second highest valuation in the parish after that of Peter Lloyd, for the second instalment of the 1543 Subsidy, while the annual value of the lands of his father, Watkin ap Thomas, was assessed at £5. The family clearly possessed extensive lands in Norton parish, for in 1572 the Impton estate, consisting of the house, one barn, two orchards, 200 acres of (arable?) land, 40 acres of meadow, 200 acres of pasture, 200 acres of wood, and 300 acres of 'furze and heath', was sold to John Flower of Norton St Philip in Somerset, along with much of the tithes of the parish.[6]

Norton St Philip was an important cloth centre with four fairs a year for the sale of wool, cloth and sheep and the Flower family had become influential in the town after leasing the grange from the prior of Hinton Abbey in 1523.[7] John Flower may have purchased Impton in order to gain a foothold in the booming cloth manufacturing centre of Presteigne where John Beddoes had already made his fortune. In 1584 Peter Watkins, the son of Thomas ap Watkin, disposed of further property in Norton to John Flower: 5 dwellings, 5 gardens, 100 acres of land, 15 acres of meadow, 20 acres of pasture, 10 acres of woodland and 300 acres of furze and heath. In 1591 John Flower sought to reinforce the status of his family by arranging the marriage of his son Edward to Elizabeth Jenkins of Dolley, whose father's estate included extensive lands in Norton parish. Admission to the higher echelons of Radnorshire society finally came in 1625 when John Flower's grandson (?) Richard was pricked as high sheriff of the county – by convention, the Crown's choice of sheriff was indicated by pricking the favoured name on a parchment bearing the names of three eligible candidates for the appointment.[8]

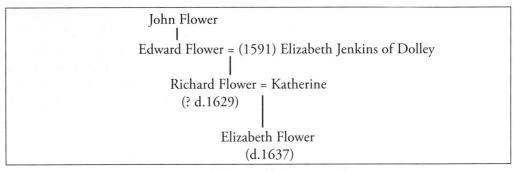

Figure 2: A Flower of Norton genealogy.
(Sources: PCAO, Deeds relating to Old Impton, Norton, 1536-1696,
and a transcription of Richard Flower's will in the papers of John and Esther Roberts)

Though the greater part of the former Mortimer lands in Radnorshire remained in the hands of the Crown until the 1820s, two of the manors, Norton and Cefnllys, passed into private hands in the course of the 16th century. How and when this happened in the case of Norton is far from clear.

Crown estate records show that at some point in the 16th century a William Horne received a grant of the manor from the Crown, though the reason for this is not clear. It seems likely that William Horne was a member of a prominent London merchant family who, in the later 15th century, had provided a high sheriff and lord mayor of the city of London. The daughter of a Robert Horne became the third wife of Sir William Norreys or Norris, a prominent supporter of Henry VII. Though his grandson, Sir Henry Norris, was executed in 1536 as an alleged lover of Anne Boleyn, the wife of Henry VIII, the family continued to have considerable influence at the courts of Edward VI, Mary and Elizabeth I. Sir Henry's brother, Sir John Norris, served Henry VIII, Edward VI and Mary, while Sir Henry's son, Sir Edward Norris, was a favourite of Elizabeth I.[9] Almost certainly it was this high status Norris connection which enabled the Horne family to secure the grant of the manor of Norton from the Crown, though there is no documentary evidence to support this contention.

Nor is it clear when the Hornes acquired the manor, though it seems likely to have been no earlier than the reign of Edward VI. W.H. Howse maintained that it was in the hands of Richard Blackbache in the reign of Henry VIII and that he left it to his son Roger in 1545, but his assertion seems to have been based on a misreading of a clause in the abstract of Richard Blackbache's will of September 1545. He interprets the clause 'To Roger Blackbache, eldest son, all lands at Blackbache and lordship of Norton afsd' to mean that Roger was to have Blackbache <u>and</u> the lordship of the manor of Norton, rather than that he was to receive Blackbache and all other lands of Richard's in the lordship of Norton. Certainly the Blackbache family, seated in Norton, appear to have lacked the wealth, the status and connections at the royal court needed to acquire the lordship from the Crown.[10]

In 1563 William Horne conveyed the manor to John Tamworth, c.1524-69, the MP for Boston in the Parliament of 1563, a trusted servant of Elizabeth I whom he served in a variety of posts including clerk of Windsor Castle, groom of the privy chamber and keeper of the privy purse. Tamworth married a sister of Sir Francis Walsingham, Elizabeth I's spymaster general, and was thought to have puritan sympathies and may have spent the years of Mary I's reign abroad. He used much of the money gained from his royal appointments to speculate in land and the lordship of the manor of Norton was an investment of this type. It did not necessitate his presence in the locality, for it could be managed by

Date	Change in ownership
1563	The manor conveyed to John Tamworth by William Horne
1624	Ownership of one-third of the manor descended to Christopher Tamworth
1626	This third of the manor conveyed to George Dalston
1634	John Powell purchased the whole manor from George Dalston, Bridget Mullins and Elizabeth Reresby
1640	Samuel Powell inherited the manor from his father
1654	Samuel Powell sold the manor to his half-brother James
1682	The manor transferred to Robert Powell, mercer, of Worcester and his wife Joyce
1693	Joyce Creed, widow of Robert Powell, sold the manor to Littleton Powell
1713	Littleton Powell sold the manor to Thomas Harley of Kinsham Court

Figure 3: Ownership of the manor of Norton.
(Source: The Harley papers, Brampton Bryan, Bundle 58)

a steward who could rent out the demesne (the land normally farmed by the lord of the manor) and collect the rents, fees and fines due from the tenants and freeholders. In his will Tamworth left the lordship of Norton, with the tithes and the advowson – the right to appoint the parish priest – to be divided equally between his daughters, Bridget and Elizabeth, and a Christopher Tamworth, probably a nephew or godson.[11]

3   STUART NORTON

The opening 30 years or so of the 17th century saw some of the old certainties of the later Tudor age in east Radnorshire evaporate. Inflation, conspicuous consumption and generous patronage, all considered essential to maintain local political influence, saw the Monaughty branch of the Price family and the Presteigne branch of the Bradshaws in great financial difficulties, a situation which undermined their social standing and political influence.

In Norton the status quo was also open to challenge on the death of Mistress Elizabeth Flower in 1637 – her memorial stone may be seen in the sanctuary of St Andrew's – upon which the Norton branch of the family seems to have come to an end, possibly as a result of deaths in three successive generations within less than 40 years. Despite Richard Flower's elevation to the shrievalty in 1625 the family seems never to have made its impact upon the locality that might have been expected. This may well have stemmed from the disastrous effects on the Presteigne cloth industry of the plague epidemics of 1593 and 1610 which caused 343 and between 115 and 125 deaths respectively in the town, and gave little incentive to invest.[1]

However the Flower family were incomers and it is likely that the collapse of the Lloyd family of Boultibrooke in the second decade of the 17th century made a much greater impact since the family, in alliance with the Prices of Monaughty and the Bradshaws of Presteigne, had dominated eastern Radnorshire for the best part of a century.

The waning in the standing of the Lloyds stemmed in part from the impact of inflation and plague upon their resources which were markedly smaller than those of their patrons-cum-allies, and matters were not helped by the large number of dependents which these relatively slender resources had to maintain in a manner in keeping with their social status.

In 1610 Peter Lloyd found his authority challenged in his own parish by Edward Flower and Brian Crowther, a prominent lawyer at the Court of the Council of Wales and the Marches, who also owned land in Norton. Peter Lloyd had been appointed collector of the mise – a gift of money from each county to a new king at his accession – which James I did not decide to collect until 1610. Crowther publicly opposed its payment on the grounds that it was too late to levy a mise. After an assault on Lloyd and his followers near Boultibrooke by Crowther, Flower and their supporters, Lloyd took his complaint to the Court of Star Chamber, but the outcome of the case is not known. In the next few years Peter Lloyd's second son and ultimate heir found himself in such financial difficulties that in 1612-13 he was forced to sell outlying portions of the family estate, a meadow at Paradise to the south of Presteigne township and Inaston, a field to the south-east of Presteigne, to Nicholas Taylor of Presteigne, a rising lawyer at the Court of the Council of Wales and the Marches.[2]

By 1620 Boultibrooke was no longer in Lloyd hands. In 1619 John Read of London and freeman of the Company of Brown Bakers had purchased the Bradshaw estate in Presteigne in 1619 for his son John Read junior, and in 1620 the latter also seems to have owned Boultibrooke, for at that date it was the residence of Read's sister Elinor and her husband John Strachan. The noted Radnorshire historian R.C.B. Oliver suggested that John Read junior may have married Benet or Benedicta – the daughter and heir of John Lloyd, the oldest son of Peter Lloyd – who had brought with her Boultibrooke as her dowry. However, with no documentary evidence for the marriage to support this theory, Oliver was prepared to accept that Read may simply have purchased the Boultibrooke estate from the financially embarrassed Lloyd family.[3]

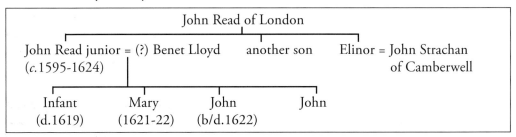

Figure 4: A Read family genealogy
(Source: PCAO, RCB Oliver's draft article on John Read)

Neither Boultibrooke nor the Manor House remained in the hands of the Read family for long. Following the death of John Read junior in 1624 both estates passed into the hands of Griffith Jones, an ambitious Presteigne lawyer who was one of John Read's executors and who may have used his position to obtain the properties on favourable terms. Jones served as high sheriff of Radnorshire in 1628 but was murdered during his year of office whereupon his property passed to his brother and heir, Evan Jones. On the latter's death the family properties passed to his son Richard who, Mr Oliver claimed, married Anne, the daughter of James Price of Monaughty.

Since Price, the son of Evan Jones, had died childless, the estate passed to his sisters, Bridget receiving Boultibrooke, and Elizabeth the Presteigne estate. Though twice married, Bridget died childless in 1687 and Boultibrooke passed to Elizabeth, who had married Edward Price of Glanmeheli in the parish of Kerry, Montgomeryshire in 1666. Edward Price, by virtue of his wife's estates, and the prestige of his Montgomeryshire family, seemed destined to play a prominent role in Radnorshire affairs: he was added to the Radnorshire Bench in 1671, served as colonel of the Brecon and Radnor joint militia between 1689 and 1697 and served as high sheriff in 1700.

However, his career was not without difficulties as he seems to have been continually in debt. Moreover, his loyalty to William III, brought to power by the Glorious Revolution of 1688, was questioned in the early 1690s when he lost a case for damages in the House

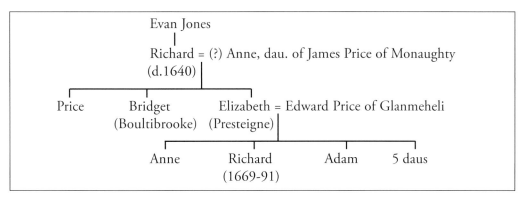

Figure 5: A genealogy of the Jones family of Presteigne.
(Source: R.C.B. Oliver, 'The Hartstonges and Radnorshire Part II' TRS 1974, p.31)

of Lords, following an accusation that he 'was disaffected from the Government'. He lost his place on the Commission of the Peace as a result of these suspicions, which may also explain why, though pricked as high sheriff for Radnorshire in November 1693, he was replaced by Robert Curtler in 1694. His appointment as high sheriff in 1700, however, suggests that by then suspicions of his disloyalty had evaporated.[4]

In April 1703 Price was attacked by Thomas Baskerville of Bryngwyn in Presteigne and suffered a deep wound in the groin, from which he died the following day.[5] This may have been the event which gave rise to the story told by W.H. Howse in his *Presteigne Past and Present* of the duel between a 'James Baskerville of Aberedw' and a 'Colonel Lloyd' in the Old Oak Inn in Broad Street as a result of a quarrel arising from a cockfight – Colonel Bell Lloyd was a subsequent owner of Boultibrooke.

Another family of some influence in 17th-century Norton was the Lewis family of Upper Dolley, a cadet branch of the Lewis family of Harpton, descended from Charles Lewis, the fourth son of Thomas Lewis (1519-1606). The house, described by Richard Suggett as 'an elaborate, jettied, timber-framed 16th century' building, gives an indication of the wealth of the Lewis family, though it never played as significant a role in the parish as one might have expected.[6] In the first place the major estates of this branch of the Lewis family lay in the Walton, Newcastle and Kinnerton area rather than in Norton – significantly the son of Charles Lewis was known as Hugh Lewis of Hindwell. Moreover this Hugh Lewis appears to have been in chronic financial difficulties since he was constantly mortgaging parts of the family estate. His son Charles, 'being imbued in debt and very idle and extravagant', mortgaged, remortgaged and finally sold most of the estate before decamping to Ireland *c.*1710, where he found a position with the Commissioners of the Revenue of Ireland which brought him 'but poor bread'.[7]

John Tamworth's division of the lordship into three lasted until 1634, though Christopher Tamworth had died in 1626. On his death his third of the lordship reverted to the Crown and Charles I conveyed it to Sir George Dalston, a courtier and MP for Cumberland. In 1634 John Powell united the manor, buying Dalston's third for £360, and those of John Tamworth's daughters, Bridget, now Mrs William Mullins, and Elizabeth, now the widow of Sir George Reresby.[8]

John Powell was the grandson of Walter Powell of Bucknell and a Merchant Adventurer 'of London and Hamburg', who had made a fortune in the Baltic trade and who had returned to the Radnor-Shropshire-Herefordshire border to build up a large landed estate. He had purchased Stanage in 1633, prior to this living at Willey Hall. He served as High Sheriff of Radnorshire 1639-40 and was appointed a colonel in the Royalist forces on the outbreak of the Civil War in 1642 but did not take an active part in the conflict. His oldest son Samuel (1624-86) was born in Hamburg and was naturalized when the family returned to London in 1628. He was also appointed a colonel in the Royalist army in 1642 despite his youth, and during the Second Civil War of 1648 he was suspected of being implicated in the Herefordshire rising led by Sir Henry Lingen. However he escaped punishment at the hands of the Parliamentarians thanks to some judicious bribery and by playing off the Herefordshire officials against their Radnorshire counterparts.[9]

In 1654 Samuel Powell sold the manor to his half-brother James, the oldest son of his father's second marriage to Elizabeth Walmsley, the daughter of a London merchant, for £200. In 1663 when Robert Powell, a mercer of Worcester and the oldest son of James Powell, married Joyce, the daughter of Humphrey Longmore, the mayor of Worcester, the manor of Norton was settled on her for life in return for her dowry of £800. After the death of Robert Powell, Joyce married Charles Creed in 1679 and in 1693 sold the manor to Samuel Powell's second son, Littleton, one of the six Clerks of Chancery. In 1713 Littleton Powell sold the manor to Thomas Harley of Kinsham Court, for £1,031 10 shillings.[10]

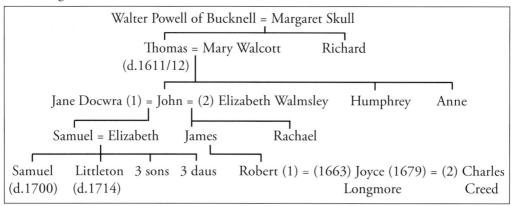

Figure 6: A concise Powell genealogy
(Source: John Burke, A Genealogical and Heraldic History of the Commoners of Great Britain.
N.b. The identification of Robert Powell as the son of James Powell
must be considered as speculative)

Management of the Manor

The conveyance of 1626 granting one-third of the manor to Sir George Dalston described the manor as consisting of 40 messuages, 2 mills, 40 gardens, 500 acres of arable, 200 acres of meadow, 4,000 acres of pasture and 200 acres of heath.[11] This was a gross over-estimate since the manor, which included the whole parish, amounted to 3,144 acres. The lord of the manor initially received rents in kind, usually fowls and eggs at Christmas and Easter along with a small money rent from the customary tenants, the copyholders, who held their lands on a long lease, usually for three lives. Freeholders in the manor paid a chief rent, a small annual residual rent levied on each property.[12]

On the death of a copyholder or freeholder, a 'heriot' consisting of his best beast was due to the lord, together with a 'relief', usually less than 10 shillings. A heriot was also levied on the sale of a property and a new tenant or owner, heir or purchaser, was also liable to pay a relief. Offenders who allowed livestock to stray, failed to keep gates of hedges in repair, enclosed part of the common grazing, or failed to fence in their holdings in the open fields before 29 September, when winter corn was to be sown, or before 13 February in the case of spring corn, were 'presented' before the manorial court and fined if the offence was proven.

The administration of the manor was in the hands of the steward, appointed by the lord, assisted by the bailiff and jury elected by the tenants at the manorial court which was held twice a year. Those who failed to attend at least one meeting of the court in a year were fined – in 1608, 2 shillings and 6 pence in the case of a freeholder, a shilling in the case of a tenant, and 3 pence in the case of a servant. The court dealt with three types of business: property transactions within the manor; breaches of manorial regulations and customs; and minor breaches of the law. The decisions of the court were enforced by the petty constable for the parish, elected yearly by the court. This post was not sought after and in 1698 William Phillips was fined 3 shillings and 11 pence for refusing the post. The revenue which the lord received from fees, fines, rents and dues depended upon the efficiency of the steward and in the case of 17th-century Norton, would probably have amounted to between £70 and £80 a year.

17th-century manorial rolls	1845 tithe map
Crawling field	Minns Field
Brook field	Furlongs field and Furlongs at Townsend
Chessell field	Chissell field
Longland field	Upper Long fields
Lower field	Little Norton field

Figure 7: The Norton open fields in the 17th and 19th centuries.
(Source: TRS 1967*, pp.24-26)*

Working backwards from the residual open field system shown on the tithe map of 1845 and with the aid of the manorial rolls of the late 17th century, Dr Dorothy Sylvester was able to identify and name the open arable fields or groups of fields worked originally on some variant of the three year rotation of wheat or barley, oats and then fallow.[13] One possibility she suggests is that Furlongs field and Furlongs at Townsend (Brookfield) formed part of, or were worked with Chissell field to the east of Norton Brook; Crawling or Minns Field formed the second field and that Longland Field and Lower Field (Upper

Long Fields and Little Norton Field) formed the third field which may have extended originally further south towards the Lugg. The tithe survey plan of Norton of 1845 shows that some of the plots of land in the open fields consisted of a single quillet – a long narrow strip of land – or a group of quillets, which had survived virtually intact since at least the 17th century.

Dr Sylvester's identification of the manor's meadowland and open common pasture is more tentative. She suggests that the meadowland may have been located to the south of the Lugg, on land then in Norton parish, and also along Norton Brook, to the north of the settlement as far as Hares Green, with the open common pasture lying on the uplands to the west, north and east of the settlement, a 'bridge-shaped area', much above 1,000 feet, and including parts of Hawthorn Hill, Stonewall Hill and Llanwen Hill.

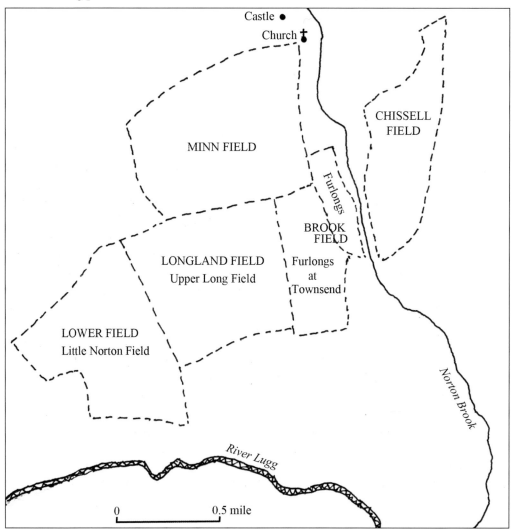

Figure 8: Norton's open fields.
(Source: Dorothy Sylvester's map facing p.24, TRS 1967

18

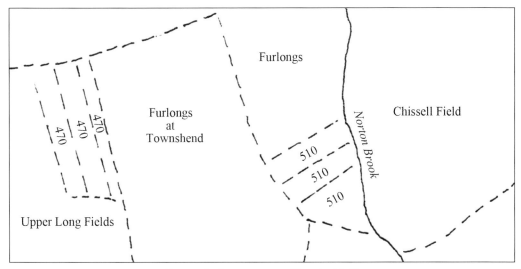

Figure 9: Surviving quillets in 1845.
(Source: Norton Tithe Survey map, 1845)

Norton and the Civil War

Radnorshire was Royalist in its sympathies, at least during the opening years of the war, and there is no documentary evidence of any military action in the Norton area which would explain the discovery in the fabric of the church tower, at the time of the church restoration in 1868, of a 12 pound cannon ball and the marks of several other similar missiles.[14] After the Parliamentarian raid on Presteigne on the night of 27-28 October 1642, the Presteigne-Knighton area experienced a period of quiet until the two Royalist attacks on the Parliamentarian enclave of Brampton Bryan of July-September 1643 and October 1643-April 1644. The Brampton Bryan campaigns were followed by another period of uneasy peace, broken during the late summer and early autumn of 1645 when Parliamentarian forces took control of the Presteigne-Knighton area. It seems likely that the damage to the church tower occurred during this last period of hostilities in the locality.

Once in control of the county, it was Parliamentarian policy to live off the land as far as possible, requisitioning supplies from the local population. Thus in January 1646 Norton was called upon to provide 20 bushels of oats, a wagonload of hay, 112 pounds of bread, 60 pounds of cheese, 20 pounds of butter and 40 pounds of beef and bacon for the troops garrisoned at Presteigne. On two occasions the parish was required to provide teams of horses to carry turf and timber from Stapleton and Norton respectively. In addition Norton was also required to provide free board and lodging for detachments of troops for varying periods, never more than nine days, in 1646, and to finance the Parliamentarian war effort by paying a three monthly assessment of £11 and 4 shillings, backdated to May 1645.[15]

Church and community

Of the fabric of St Andrew's in this period we know little save that parts of the bell-tower may date from the 17th century. It was built to house the two bells, one inscribed SOLI DEO GLORIA dated either 1638 or 1659, the other inscribed WILLIAM TAYLOR

HIGH SHERIFF 1687. This was probably the William Taylor who, with five other youths, rode off to join the forces of Charles II at the battle of Worcester on 3 September 1651.[16] Fortunately for Taylor and his associates, their families possessed sufficient local influence to repeatedly delay the hearing of their cases before the local Parliamentarian court and although the final outcome is unknown, it seems likely they avoided punishment for their escapade.

Of the incumbents, little is known beyond their names and then only from 1563. Since Brian Jones, rector of New Radnor in the 1970s, in accordance with Anglican tradition names only those clergy ordained and instituted according to canon law, there is a question mark over the long tenure attributed to Hugh Jones, given the turmoil of the Civil War and Interregnum. However, in light of the 40-year incumbency of Roger Howell and the 52-year incumbency of Richard Vaughan, Hugh Jones' long tenure cannot be considered exceptional.

1563	John Morrys	1623	Hugh Jones
1572	Roger Powell	1666	Thomas Warburton
1576	Roger Howell	1684	William Tristram
1616	Henry George	1704	Richard Vaughan

Figure 10: Norton Incumbents 1563-1704.
(Source: Revd. Brian Jones The Churches of the Knighton Deanery,
and Bishop's Transcripts, Norton parish, 1666 and 1684, HCRO)

The records of the church courts of the Hereford diocese gives us occasional glances into some aspects of life in Norton in the 17th century, usually by no means as lurid as the tangled love life of Anna Goch recounted earlier, since the jurisdiction of the church courts had declined significantly. Most of the citations involving Norton parishioners in the 1670s were relatively mundane – failure to pay tithes, church dues known as the lewn (the church rate), playing tennis against the wall of the church, or failing to attend church or to take communion – possible indications of non-conformist sympathies. The Church remained an arbiter of public morality however, thus in Norton in 1677 Edward Grenous was ordered to perform public penance for fornication with a Jane Watkins. Citations could be made by individual parishioners and were sometimes false, motivated by spite or unreliable gossip. Thus in 1673 two Norton parishioners, Thomas Lloyd and Bridget Williams, cited for incontinency – having a sexual relationship outside marriage – were able to refute the charge and assert their innocence.[17]

Based on the data given in the conveyance of one-third of the manor to Dalston in 1626 and the number of houses in the parish in the Hearth Tax return of 1670 and using a conventional multiplier of 5, the population of the parish in the mid-17th century was probably about 175.[18] The return also shows the parish to have 35 houses, 21 with one hearth, 8 with two hearths, 2 with three hearths, 1 with four hearths and 3 (Boultibrooke, Impton and Upper Dolley?) with five hearths. Norton in 1670 also appears to have been one of the wealthier Radnorshire parishes in terms of the percentage of houses with more than one hearth (40%) and the average number of hearths per house (1.77). This hearth/house ratio was much higher than the average for any of the Radnorshire Hundreds and for Radnorshire as a whole (1.41) and virtually on a par with the Herefordshire average of 1.78 hearths. Even so it was essentially an agricultural community, with the parish register usually describing males buried in the church yard as yeomen.

The borough of Norton

Norton manorial roll makes reference to 'the manor and borough of Norton' in 1687 and 1688. The timing of this claim to borough status is intriguing since the 1680s was a time of constitutional crisis; first the accession of the Catholic James II to the throne in 1685, and then his overthrow in the 'Glorious Revolution' of 1688. In Radnorshire the crisis took the form of a controversy as to which places had the right to vote in an election of an MP to represent the Radnor Boroughs. In the disputed election of 1690, Rowland Gwynne claimed that the right to vote lay not only with the freemen of the boroughs of New Radnor, Cefnllys, Knighton, Knucklas and Rhayader, all of whom regularly voted, but also with the freemen of the boroughs of Painscastle, Presteigne and possibly Norton.[19]

Though the House of Commons found against Gwynne, Norton clung firmly to its claim to borough status, though no document granting such a status has come to light. In his *Topographical Dictionary of Wales* of 1833, Samuel Lewis reported that the inhabitants of Norton referred to the place as a borough and to themselves as burgesses, though the privileges this brought were few and ill-

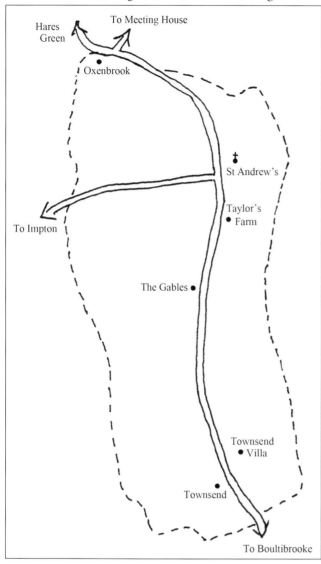

Figure 11: The old borough of Norton.
(Source: The papers of John and Esther Roberts)

defined. This claim to borough status could well be dismissed as a conceit, were it not for a statement in the Tithe Commutation Schedule of 1845 to the effect that:

> The Vicar of the said parish is entitled to all the tithes of Corn Grain and Hay arising from all the lands of the said parish situate within a certain district called the Borough of Norton, which district is well known by Metes and Bounds which lands contain by estimation 45 acres.[20]

The precise boundaries of the borough are not known, but John and Esther Roberts, assuming that the borough would cover the heart of the village, have used the tithe commutation schedule and map to chart its possible location, which they suggest may have stretched along both sides of the present B4355 from Oxenbrook to the north of the village to Townsend Villa to the south.

4   18TH-CENTURY NORTON

The 18th century appears to have been a time of stagnation in both Presteigne and Knighton, characterised by slow population growth, and one senses the same inertia and lack of dynamism in 18th-century Norton, though here it seems to have stemmed from the dominance of non-resident landlords. The Montgomeryshire owners of Boultibrooke, the Prices and then Bell Lloyd, were concerned primarily with matters in that county, and in the remainder of the parish the Harleys at Kinsham Court and Brampton Bryan extended their influence and dominated the local land market. The lack of a resident gentry meant that the relationship between landlord and tenant became much more impersonal and the sense of a common allegiance to the parish on the part of both landlord and tenants was eroded.

The parochial assessments for the poor rate in 1710 and the church rate or lewn levied in 1723 to raise funds 'towards the repayring of the church' enable an impression to be gained of the pattern of landholding in the parish. Such rates were levied upon the occupier, who was not necessarily the owner, and the assessments were based upon the annual value of each holding, not on the acreage. Nor do the assessments reflect the actual annual commercial value of the holdings, they were conventional assessments drawn up by the churchwardens to allocate the financial burden equitably between property occupiers in the parish. The two assessments show the parish to have two very large estates, three large farms, five or so medium sized farms, ten smaller farms, ten smallholdings and fifteen or so holdings consisting of a cottage, garden and possibly a small plot of land, or simply a plot of land. A comparison of the 1710 with 1723 rate assessments and other rate and Land Tax assessments of the early 1720s suggests that some slight downward movement had taken place in the valuation of

	1710 Poor rate	1723 Church rate
Annual value	Number assessed	Number assessed
£60 or more	2	2
£30 or more	3	3
£20 or more	5	2
£10 or more	10	10
£5 or more	10	11
Under £5	17	18

Figure 12: Property assessments in Norton, 1710 and 1723.
(Source: Harley Papers at Brampton Bryan, Bundle 1, 1/83 and 1/92
N.b. The annual value of the lordship of the manor is not included in either column)

some medium and smaller properties in the second decade of the 18th century, though this may indicate attempts to reduce liability to pay.[1]

In these early 18th-century poor rate and Land Tax assessments, holdings are sometimes referred to by the name of the occupier rather than by the name of the property. Even so some properties had names still in use today, though the size of the holding may have changed. The date given after the name of the property indicates the year of the assessment cited.

Annual valuation of £60+	Impton (1710) Boultibrooke (1710)
Annual valuation of £30+	'Mr Taylor's estate' – Taylor's Farm? (1710), The Farm (1710), 'Thos. Carter, gent' – Carter's Farm? (1710)
Annual valuation of £20+	Townsend (1710 – divided into two holdings)
Annual valuation of £10+	Stocking-Stocken (1710), Hares Green (1725)
Annual valuation of £5+	The Hazels (1710)
Annual valuation of less than £5:	Cook's House (1710) or Cooks Land (1720) The Elvels/The Elvins (1725), Badge – Bach farm? (1725)

Other properties named in early 18th-century assessments now have a different name or have been absorbed into other holdings:

Annual valuation of £10+	Sholton (1710)
Annual valuation of £5+	Lysevern (1710) Red Leys (1710) and Estop (1710)
Annual valuation of less than £5:	The Slade (1710) Whitehouse (1710), The Pikes (1710), Lloyds and Bettys (1710), Hollands Lawn (1716), Redmind (1720), Upper Newton (1710)

Some of these holdings were still in existence at the time of the Tithe Survey of 1845, while others were recalled only as field names. Thus in 1845 Lysevern was a holding of 51 acres and Hollands Lawn was a smallholding of 15 acres. Fields named Newton Field were to be found on Taylor's Farm, Corns, now called Orchard House, then a smallholding of nearly 28 acres, and on Lysevern. A field known as Red Leys Field was to be found on Hill House and Slad Field on Taylor's Farm.

Boultibrooke in the 18th century

For almost the whole of the century Boultibrooke remained in the possession of Montgomeryshire gentry families and for most of this time was in the hands of tenants.

Following his marriage to the 15-year-old Mary Kyffin, Adam Price settled at Bodfach Hall, Llanfylin, where his High Church views and Jacobite sympathies led to him inciting a mob to burn down the dissenters' meeting house in Llanfylin at the time of the Jacobite Rebellion of 1715. The son of the marriage, Edward Price inherited the Bodfach, Glanmehli and Boultibrooke estates, though like his father, he styled himself as 'of Bodfach'. Both served as high sheriff of Radnorshire, Adam in 1707 and Edward in 1741.[2]

Edward's third daughter and ultimate heiress, Anne, married Bell Lloyd of Pontrif, Flintshire, in 1758. He too settled at Bodfach which he transformed, rebuilding the house itself, building the coach house and creating extensive parkland around the house as a result

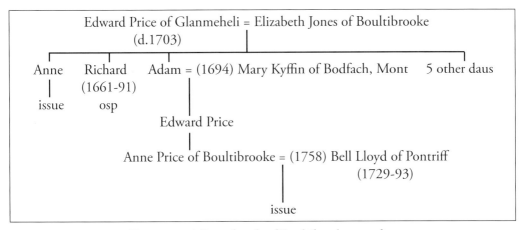

Figure 13: A Price family of Boultibrooke genealogy
(Sources: R.C.B. Oliver, 'The Hartstongues and Radnorshire Part II', TRS 1974, p.31
and www.bodfachtrust.org.uk/hisory_of_bodfach_ hall)

of buying some of Llanfylin's common land after its enclosure and draining it. He also played an active part in the public life of both Montgomeryshire and Radnorshire, serving as colonel of the Montgomeryshire militia and as high sheriff of Montgomeryshire in 1784 and of Radnorshire in 1788. His ambitious schemes may well have over-extended him financially, for he died in the King's Bench debtors' prison in London in 1793.[3]

Though most of the present house and gardens dates from the 19th century, sufficient fragments of the earlier house and grounds survive to suggest that the Montgomeryshire owners of Boultibrooke in the late 17th and the 18th century had already transformed the 16th-century farmhouse of the Lloyd family into a gentleman's residence.

Following the death of Bell Lloyd, the Boultibrooke estate was offered for sale and from the advertisements in the *Hereford Journal* of 1796 and 1797 it can be seen to have consisted of Boultibrooke House, Boultibrooke Farm and Stocking Farm and a water grist mill, in all 350 acres in Norton, let for £360, together with other farms, amounting to rather more than 390 acres in Llananno, Llanbister and Llanbadarn Fynydd.[4]

The Price family of Knighton and Impton
The Knighton branch of the Price family, which was to dominate 19th-century Norton, may first have shown an interest in the parish in 1700, for in October of that year Littleton Powell wrote to his steward Thomas Owen that if 'Mr Price' was prepared to give £1,200 for the Lordship he would 'be pleased to deal with him'.[5] The family became directly involved in the affairs of the parish in 1721 when John Price became the steward of the manor of Norton for Thomas Harley of Kinsham Court, the lord of the manor. John Price I (d.1727) and his son John Price II (d.1774) were attorneys who also acted as land agents The latter was thus well placed to advise his son, Richard Price (d.1797) when he was admitted to the tenements of Impton and Bromley in the manor of Norton in September 1766.[6] However, like the owners of Boultibrooke, the Prices were absentee owners and the parish continued to lack the leadership which traditionally came from its 'big houses'.

Population trends

In a parish such as Norton, with a population of between 175 and 200 and the number of baptisms and of burials in each year normally in single figures, the use of parish register data or bishop's transcripts to gain an insight into population trends is fraught with problems. Any conclusions reached, however broad, are highly tentative. With that caveat, over the 18th century baptisms exceeded burials in Norton by 200 or so, with the greatest excess of baptisms over burials coming in the periods 1721-40 and 1781-1800, numbering 59 and 49 respectively. This would suggest that the population may have grown significantly over the century. However, since the population of the parish in the 1801 was 221, it is clear that a significant proportion of the natural increase in population had migrated from the parish. Given that agriculture provided almost all the employment in the parish, such outward migration was inevitable.

Given the small annual numbers of burials recorded, it is difficult to detect the possible impact of epidemics in the parish. The number of burials in the parish reached double figures in 1738 and 1741 which may reflect the much higher than normal mortality in Presteigne in 1741, and the smallpox epidemic which led to high mortality in Knighton in 1742.[7] The number again reached double figures in 1789 and 1793, but this may well have stemmed from the sharp rise in food prices in the closing decades of the century.

The parish register also gives some insight into the occupations pursued by the male parishioners. In the early decades of the century, apart from the occasional 'gent' or 'esq' and craftsmen such as millers, wheelwrights, blacksmiths, and later, weavers, most male parishioners were styled 'yeoman'. However, by the middle decades, the 1740s and 1750s, an increasing number were designated 'labourers'. This may be no more than a change in terminology, but it may imply that some of the poorer parishioners were selling the small plots they possessed in the open fields and becoming landless labourers.

Church and community

Given that the parish was small and not particularly wealthy, the incumbents of the living in the 18th century seem to have been surprisingly well qualified, since four of the five were graduates of Oxford University. Tristram graduated from Jesus College in 1677; Vaughan graduated from Brasenose in 1702; Middleton Jones of Lincoln College, graduated in Civil Law in 1754; while Richard Smith may have been the student of that name at Christ Church who graduated BA in 1751 and MA in 1754.

Two of the four had close Radnorshire connections. Tristram hailed from 'Waythett' – probably Weythell – and seems to have resigned from the Norton living following his

1684	William Tristram BA
1704	Richard Vaughan BA
1756	Middleton Jones Ll B
1776	Richard Lloyd
1797	Richard Smith MA

Figure 14: Norton incumbents 1684-1797.
(Source: Norton parish register)

appointment to Llanfihangel-nant-melan in 1703. Richard Vaughan was the son of John Vaughan of Nantmel. Richard Smith may also have been a Radnorshire man, possibly the son of a William Smith of Presteigne. Middleton Jones may also have had some slight acquaintance with Radnorshire for he was a son of John Jones of Cribbarth, Breconshire. However of Richard Lloyd nothing is known.[8]

In order to exercise a measure of supervision over parishes in a diocese the church authorities issued a questionnaire on a triennial basis to the churchwardens in each parish relating to the conduct of clergy, parochial officers and the laity, the pattern of worship and the maintenance of the parish church and other church property. The churchwardens' answers to the articles of inquiry in 1719 paint Norton as a model parish with Richard Vaughan the vicar, the church officers and the laity fulfilling their responsibilities to the letter.[9] The fabric of the church was well maintained and Vaughan was carrying out his duties conscientiously. Prayers were held at 8am each Sunday and Evensong was held at 3pm between February and November, but between November and February only Morning Prayers were held. Communion was celebrated six times 'or thereabouts' a year. Vaughan catechised the children of the parish each Sunday from the beginning of March until mid-summer.

The parish had only one nonconformist family – Presbyterians – who held a service at their home. As for the parishioners in general, the churchwardens asserted confidently that no-one in the parish

Plate 2: The tower, St Andrew's Church
(Courtesy of George Lancett)

liveth under a common form of adultery, fornication or incest or that is a common swearer, drunkard or a blasphemer of God's Holy Name or Word.

They also claimed that no parishioner followed 'their calling and worldly employment' on a Sunday. The churchwardens may well have been trying to please the diocesan authorities, for their answers would seem too good to be true.

However, even if there had been a high degree of social cohesion in the parish in 1720, this had evaporated by 1740 if a letter from Vaughan to an unknown senior cleric in the Hereford diocese is taken at face value.[10] Vaughan was deeply concerned at the number of illegitimate children, six in all, that he had baptised between 1737 and 1740. Moreover, although these illegitimate births had been reported to the Church authorities by the churchwardens, no action had been taken. One mother had threatened the Norton parish officers that if they caused her trouble, she would supply them with more illegitimate children! Vaughan was also concerned at a tendency for couples to co-habit rather than to marry. He attributed all these irregularities to the high cost of marriage licences, at least £1 7 shillings (£1 35p) – more than a month's pay for a farm labourer. He claimed that 'the Poorer Sort think it a disparagement to be married by Banns, though they cannot purchase a Licence at so dear a rate'.

An examination of the parish register tends to bear out Vaughan's assertions. While the baptism of an illegitimate child every two or three years was not unusual, six baptisms of illegitimate children in a four-year period was exceptional. Again, in the period 1730-1740, of the 22 marriages in St Andrew's 10 were by banns and 12 by licence, but more strikingly, nine of the marriages involved both bride and groom from parishes other than Norton. Marriage seems to have been going out of fashion in the parish.

The remainder of the letter suggests that the relationship between Vaughan and his parishioners had broken down completely for he claimed

> Half the parishioners seldom frequent Divine Service and do not receive the sacrament once in seven years. The village is full of rude children who not only meet in the Churchyard on week days to play, to climb up the Church, to break the windows etc. But even on the Lord's Day in time of Divine service often [they] make such a noise that I am scarcely to be heard in the Church. I applied to their parents and to the churchwardens, but all in vain.

The letter ends with an appeal for assistance 'to bring these illiterate, selfconceited, stiffnecked people to live in obedience to the Laws of God'. To some extent the letter seems to have been written by an elderly, conscientious clergyman, disillusioned by a failure to make as great an impact upon his parishioners as he had wished. Even so, the letter suggests that Norton was not the archetypal deeply hierarchical rural community in which everyone knew their place, partly at least because it lacked a resident squire possessing the authority to ensure that conventional proprieties were observed.

A volume recording churchwardens' meetings and parochial accounts for the period 1769-85 gives some interesting insights into the life of the parish.[11] In 1771-72 the steeple was built at a total cost of £6 16s 3d (£16 81p) with the builder, a Mr William Botwood, receiving £5 of this. The choice of the words 'building the steeple', rather than 'rebuilding' or 'repairing' it, suggests that previously the church had possessed no more than a belfry in which the bells were hung. In 1779-80 the churchwardens paid out 3s 5d (17p) for clay, lime and 6lbs of hair to plaster or to repair the plaster in the church interior. Other items of expenditure included 2s 6d (12½p) 'for the killing of foxes' and similar sums were spent on ale on 5 November and on Easter Monday, though it is not clear if this was solely for the benefit of the bell ringers.

Other items of expenditure seem surprising. Thus on 12 December 1783 the parishioners agreed

> to occulate [inoculate] the smallpox into and upon the poor belonging to the said parish of Norton, as many as is thought proper by the said parishioners.

In December 1785 it was decided to levy a rate of a penny in the pound 'to hire a person proper to teach salm [*sic*] singing to such persons as is [*sic*] belonging to the parish'. This was not as unusual as one might think for it was a practice followed in many parishes at the time. In December 1800 an agreement was reached with Thomas Ingram, a Presteigne surgeon, that in return for the sum of £7 17s 6d (£7 8½p) to care for a Norton woman in Presteigne Workhouse with a 'foul disease'.

The relief of poverty

Since the Tudor period responsibility for the relief of poverty lay with the parish which levied a rate on property within the parish to provide the necessary funds. Two groups of people had a right of settlement in the parish and were thus eligible to receive poor relief – those born in the parish and those who had lived in the parish for a year. The churchwardens had a discretionary power to relieve other paupers who were passing through the parish, though only on a short-term basis of a day or so since rate-payers expected the poor rate to be kept to a minimum.

The second half of the 18th century was a period of almost continuous warfare which led to sharp rises in food prices. Since the poor lived at no more than subsistence level, an increasing number found it necessary to seek assistance from the parish resulting in a sharp increase in expenditure upon poor relief. In 1776 in Norton this amounted to £16 14s (£16 70p), and the annual average spending on poor relief in the period 1783-85 was £36 10s 2d, an increase of nearly 220% above the level of 1776.[12]

Faced with such increases the parish authorities sought to economise, and one way of doing so was to ensure that as few incomers as possible were able to establish a right of settlement. Another strategy was to reduce the parish's potential expenditure on relief. Thus in 1785 a girl and a boy in receipt of poor relief in Norton were sent as apprentices to a Presteigne milliner and tailor, each of whom received a premium of £4. It was then decided that in future girls of 11 or more and boys of 9 or more who became charges upon the parish were to be put out as apprentices.[13] However such measures were no more than short-term expedients, and as the rise in poor relief expenditure accelerated in the opening decades of the 19th century a new approach was called for in order to bring such expenditure under control.

Norton's roads

Prior to the mid-17th century the Presteigne-Knighton road did not pass through Norton but went over Stonewall Hill. However the 1845 tithe survey plan of Norton suggests that in the Tudor and early Stuart period the parish was served by a complex system of roads, many of them around the various open fields and others, access roads within the fields themselves.

Since Tudor times the maintenance of the roads was the responsibility or the parish and each year a householder was chosen as road surveyor to supervise their maintenance, the labour provided by able-bodied householders who were to provide a maximum of six days' unpaid labour each year while each owner of arable land was to provide a wagon and a driver free of charge for four days. Such work was most unpopular and usually the road surveyor insisted upon the minimum, and was content to concentrate his efforts on the more important of the parish roads and then only to fill the deepest ruts with field stone.

In the case of Norton the most important roads were probably the road through the village; a road running from the centre of the village in a south-west direction two-thirds of the way along the present Home Farm lane and then on to Ackhill and Dolley Green; the road from the present Tollbar Cottage to Stocken and Stonewall Hill or to Stapleton and then on to Presteigne; and Meeting House Lane over Llanwen Hill and down to Knighton. Access to the markets of Presteigne and Knighton was clearly important to the farmers of Norton, while Ackhill lay only a few hundred yards from the London-Rhayader-Abersystwyth road which, until the opening decades of the 19th century ran through Discoed and Cascob. To call such tracks roads is misleading, for they were essentially unmetalled green lanes barely negotiable by people travelling on foot or on horse-

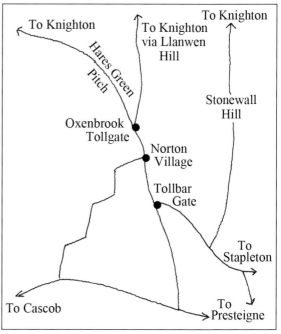

Figure 15: Norton's roads in the 18th and the early 19th centuries

back and by loads carried on sledges or panniered horses or, on the better roads, by wagons pulled by 8 or 16 horses, while in winter many were impassable for weeks if not months.

Ogilby's map shows that by 1675 the Presteigne-Knighton road ran through Norton. It crossed the Lugg by the old Boultibrooke bridge, and to avoid Boultibrooke pitch went on to Norton on the east side of Boultibrooke House, then, via Meeting House Lane, on to Knighton. However in 1775, when the Radnorshire Turnpike Trust decided to make a turnpike road between Presteigne and Knighton, it was decided to route it over the bridge in Presteigne towards Stapleton, turning to the west at the present cemetery along the lane to the present Presteigne-Norton road, through the village to Meeting House Lane at Oxenbrook and then via Llanwen Hill to Knighton.

This Stapleton route may well have been chosen because Boultibrooke bridge was in a ruinous condition in 1775 but, because the tollhouse was at Oxenbook, travellers between Presteigne and Norton escaped paying tolls. By 1780 the old Boultibrooke bridge had been rebuilt and this enabled the present road up Boultibrooke pitch to be used and in 1790 a new tollhouse was opened at the present Tollbar Cottage and the Oxenbrook tollhouse ceased to function.

Although in theory the tolls were to be used to maintain the road on which they had been collected, in practice the tolls collected by the Radnorshire Turnpike Trust were used to maintain the Aberystwyth road. Although between £30 and £40 was collected each year from travellers on the Presteigne-Knighton turnpike, the Order Book of the Trust shows no expenditure on that road until 1829-32 when £450 was spent on building the present road up Hares Green pitch, thus completing the present route between Norton and Knighton.[14]

30

5   19TH-CENTURY NORTON

The French wars of 1793-1815 cast a long shadow which was to persist long after the coming of peace in rural communities such as Norton. Even in the 1830s, long after the post-war agricultural slump, confidence in the farming community remained fragile. Even so, the re-establishment of two residential gentry families in the parish – the Jones Brydges at Boultibrooke and the (Green) Prices at Norton Manor – brought a measure of reassurance. Each house stood at the centre of a large landed estate: in 1873 the Green Prices had an estate of 8,775 acres in Radnorshire, with an estimated annual rental of £7,789, while the Boultibrooke estate amounted to 3,090 acres, 1,477 in Radnorshire and 1,613 acres in Herefordshire, with an estimated annual rental of £4,279.[1] The presence of two gentry houses in a parish with a population of between 250 and 300 meant that employment opportunities were enhanced as two sets of domestic servants and estate workers such as gardeners, grooms, carpenters and farmworkers were required.

The impact of the French Wars
The run of poor harvests in the 1790s, the threat that the country's grain imports might be disrupted and then Napoleon's attempt to block Britain's trade with Europe led to a marked rise in the price of wheat and barley and smaller rises in the prices of other agricultural goods. Increases in wages did not keep pace. Farm labourers' weekly wages did rise from 6 shillings (30p) in 1793 to 7 shillings (35p) in 1794, and to 8-10 shillings (40-50p) in winter and 9-12 shillings (45-60p) in summer in 1814, but most labourers were hired by the day and few could expect to be employed for six days a week throughout the year.[2]

Even in the best of times the labouring poor lived at or rather below subsistence level, spending more than three-quarters of their income on food, relying on expedients such as gleaning, gifts of flour on St Thomas's Day (3 July), switching to cheaper bread made from barley or muncorn (a mixture of wheat and barley) or substituting potatoes for bread to make ends meet. During the war years many of the labouring poor found it necessary to seek financial assistance from the parish, in some cases only when work was short or at those times of the year when food prices were at their highest, but in a substantial number of cases, on a regular basis. In these cases relief took the form of the payment of house rent or a small weekly cash allowance which varied according to the number of children in the family. Thus in Norton in 1803, six adults and nine children under the age of 14 were relieved on a regular basis and a further nine adults were relieved occasionally. About 11% of the parish population were in receipt of poor relief in Norton in 1803, a much lower

Year	Expenditure (£)	Year	Expenditure (£)
1800-01	133	1808-09	120
1801-02	147	1809-10	120
1802-03	49	1810-11	87
1803-04	65	1811-12	124
1804-05	70	1812-13	151
1805-06	55	1813-14	148
1806-07	101	1814-15	116
1807-08	70	1815-16	192

Figure 16: Poor relief expenditure in Norton 1800-1815 (to the nearest £).
N.b. The financial year began on Lady Day, 25 March.
(Source: PCAO R/QS/S3729)

proportion than Discoed's 35%. In Norton the poor rate was levied at 3s 9d (19p) in the pound, whereas in Discoed the rate was higher, unsurprisingly, at 8 shillings (40p) in the pound.[3] The highest expenditure on poor relief occurred in the years of high wheat prices – in 1800-02 and from 1808-09 to 1815-16.

Farmers did not gain as much as one might have expected from the rising food prices since they were also faced with rising poor rates, national taxes and tithes, while tenant farmers also had to contend with steep increases in rent. Moreover the coming of peace in 1815 led to a sharp fall in the price of agricultural products which plunged farming into crisis, since the level of rents, tithes and local taxation did not adjust immediately to the new situation.

In Norton the crisis became apparent in September 1814 when Arthur Phillips of The Hazels, unable to meet his commitments, sold his livestock, farm implements, 2 tons of hay and his standing crops of wheat, barley, oats and peas.[4] Over the next few years a number of farms in the parish were either sold – Carter's Farm, Back Lane Farm, and Green Lane Farm, all seemingly bought by Richard Price – or, like The Farm and Holland's Lawn, put up for rent. It was not in the landlord's interests to leave a holding untenanted and on occasions it was necessary to offer inducements to attract a new tenant or to persuade an existing tenant to remain. Thus in 1817 nearby Willey Hall, a farm of 400 acres, was offered for a yearly rent of £200 instead of the usual rent of £300. In 1822 Sir Harford Jones (Brydges) gave a retrospective reduction to his tenants of 10% for the last five years and a further rebate of 20% on the last two years and promised a further reduction 'if times do not mend'.[5]

By the mid-1820s the immediate post-war agricultural slump had eased thanks to a cut in national taxation, a ban on imports of foreign grain if the price of British grain fell below a given sum, and a fall in the level of farm rents. Even so farmers still felt insecure and deemed it necessary to trim costs by cutting labourers' wages and seeking to reduce poor relief expenditure. Thus by the 1830s the general level of labourers' wages in Radnorshire had fallen back to 8 shillings (40p) a week. In order to reduce poor relief expenditure the poor were farmed out to the contractor submitting the lowest tender. Thus in 1817 a Mrs Jane Dykes agreed to 'support and find the poor of the parish of Norton for 12 months' for £155. Thereafter the successful bid fell steadily, to £135 in 1823, £128 in 1829, £120 in 1830, £115 in 1831, £100 in 1833 and just £80 in 1835.[6]

Population and housing 1801-41

The population of Norton remained virtually unchanged over the first decade of the century, but between 1811 and 1821 it increased by 44%. This was not the result of natural increase, for baptisms only exceeded burials by 13 in the period 1811-20, but of in-migration. The inflow probably stemmed from three factors: the return of men from the forces after the coming of peace; the temporary inflow of labourers and their families from the surrounding countryside as a result of farmers shedding labour; and the purchase of Boultibrooke from the Harley family in 1812 by Sir Harford Jones, who assumed the additional surname of Brydges in 1826. Harford Jones was very conscious of his position and set about refurbishing the house, grounds and estate, maintaining a large staff of house servants, farmworkers, estate tradesmen and general labourers. Thereafter the population of the parish tended to level out, for the most part hovering in the 290s into the 1850s.

	Population	Occupied houses
1801	221	32
1811	216	41
1821	312	45
1831	297	56
1841	291	61

Figure 17: Population and housing 1801-41.
(Source: Printed census data)

In 1801 the housing situation in the parish was dire. Crammed into 32 houses were 53 families at an average of nearly 7 people per house. By 1821 matters had not improved, for with 58 families occupying 45 houses, the average number of people per house remained at 6.9. In practice overcrowding was not as great as these figures suggest for the two big houses and the larger farms in the parish accommodated significant numbers of domestic staff and farm servants. In the larger farms the female servants were accommodated in the attics and the male farm servants and boys in the lofts of barns and stables. The censuses of 1831-51 suggest that with a relatively stable population and an increased supply of housing the level of overcrowding was reduced. Even so, since most labourers' cottages had at most two sometimes inter-connected bedrooms, sleeping arrangements could be problematic.

The pattern of land-owning and landholding in Norton

The tithe schedule of 1845 showed Richard Price of Norton Manor to be the largest landowner in the parish with 1,429 acres, and Sir Harford Jones Brydges a poor second with 310 acres. Between them they held 76% of the land in private hands, with the remaining

24% held by a further nine proprietors. In addition to Richard Price at Norton Manor and Sir Harford Jones Brydges at Boultibrooke, there were four other owner-occupiers: Richard Edwards at Hares Green, William Monington at Bach, Thomas Partridge at The Pools and William Morgan at Ackhill. It should be noted that Ackhill and Stocking farms had extensive acreages outside Norton parish. Indeed the Stocking farmstead was in Presteigne parish, though it had a pew in Norton church.

Holding	Owner	Tenant	Acreage
Meeting House	Elizabeth Abley	James Edwards	60 acres
Corns	Elizabeth Abley	Evan Pugh	28 acres
Quarry	Sir Harford Jones Brydges	John Hughes	16 acres
Hares Green	Richard Edwards	Himself	90 acres
Lysevern	Edward Lee James	Evan Pugh	52 acres
Part of Ackhill	William Morgan	Himself	31 acres
Bach	William Monington	Himself	46 acres
The Pools	Thomas Partridge	Himself	53 acres
Norton Manor	Richard Price	Himself	307 acres
Taylor's	Richard Price	William Monington	127 acres
Back Lane	Richard Price	Edward Abley	237 acres
The Farm	Richard Price	James Price	186 acres
Hill House	Richard Price	John Deakins	243 acres
Carter's	Richard Price	Thomas Griffiths	183 acres
Greenway	Richard Price	Benjamin Plevy	7 acres
Townsend	Richard Price	James McDougal	19 acres
Cook's House	Richard Price	J. Monington & T. Clee	16 acres
Boultibrooke	Sir Harford Jones Brydges	Himself	179 acres
Lord Oxford's land	Sir Harford Jones Brydges	Himself	10 acres
Stocking	Sir Harford Jones Brydges	Thomas Galliers	106 acres
Newton's	Sir Harford Jones Brydges	John Hughes	17 acres
The Hazels and Elvins	Anne Phillips	Richard Edwards	63 acres
Blackpatch	The Beebee family	Thomas Wright	102 acres
Holland's Lawn	Richard Price	James Young	15 acres

Table 18: Norton landowners and land holders.
(Source: PCAO Norton Tithe Schedule, 1845)

In addition to Hares Green, Richard Edwards also rented The Hazels and Elvins, a total holding of 153 acres, while William Monington of Bach farm also rented Taylor's from Richard Price, making his holding 173 acres in all. John Hughes, the tenant of the Quarry, also rented Newton's from the Boultibrooke estate, the two together giving him a viable holding of nearly 33 acres. Similarly Evan Pugh, the tenant of Corns, also rented Lysevern, giving him a total holding of rather more than 79 acres. It also seems likely that 'Lord Oxford's Land', eight small parcels totalling 9.75 acres which presumably had been in Harley hands at some time, was farmed in conjunction with Boultibrooke. On the other hand, Cook's House was divided into two holdings. In all there were 19 holdings of more than 5 acres and the average holding was 106 acres, surprisingly large for a Radnorshire parish. However a more accurate picture of the structure of landholdings in the parish is to be found in the distribution of holdings by size, which shows that nearly half of the farms in the parish in 1845 were less than 100 acres.

Size of holding	No. of holdings
Over 200 acres	3
100-199 acres	7
50-99 acres	2
20-49 acres	2
19 acres and under	5

Figure 19: Holdings in Norton in 1845

In addition to their holdings the farmers of Norton also had access to more than 800 acres of common grazing land. Two large areas of commons, 143 acres in all, lay on Llanwen Hill along the northern borders of Knighton parish. Another 297 acres of commons and waste lay on Hawthorn Hill, while a further 363 acres lay on the western slopes of Stonewall Hill.[7] Farmers did not have access to all the commons and waste, but by custom were given exclusive use of waste land near to their holding. Thus the tenants of The Hazels and Elvins had grazing rights on Hawthorn Hill, those farming Hill House, the Meeting House and Carters Farm had grazing rights on Llanwen Hill, while Back Lane Farm, Blackpatch and The Farm had grazing rights on Stonewall Hill. Despite this clashes could still occur over particularly good grazing areas.

Figure 20: Norton farms of the 19th century.
Farms in italics did not exist in 1845

Norton in the mid-19th century

On the death of Richard Price in 1861 the Norton Manor estate passed to his nephew Richard Green who took the additional surname of Price. Green Price was a man of great energy and drive who promptly set about modernising the estate and expanding the village, providing a new vicarage, housing for his employees and a new school to replace the old school in the churchyard. After 30 years of marking time the parish's population and housing stock grew sharply between 1861 and 1871, by 14% and 17% respectively.

	Population	Housing stock
1841	291	65
1851	294	60
1861	313	60
1871	357	70

Figure 21: Population and housing 1841-71.
(Source: Printed census data)

The enumerators' returns for the censuses of the period enables us to build up a detailed picture of the composition and the structure of the community. If we assume that farmers' wives, their sons and daughters aged 13 or more, and domestic servants on farms played some role in the work of the farm, agriculture was easily the main source of employment in the parish. However the percentage of women and particularly of men so employed declined sharply in the 1850s and 1860s, probably as a result of increasing mechanisation of farming and possibly as a result of a shift from arable to pastoral farming. Thus by 1871 agriculture, which had provided employment for more than 70% of economically active males in Norton in 1841, 1851 and 1861, accounted for only 59% of the male labour force. In Norton the male labour force consisted of about equal proportions of farm servants who boarded at the farm and farm labourers who lived in cottages in the vicinity of the farm – unlike much of central and western Radnorshire where the great majority of farm workers lived in.

The other significant sector of male employment comprised craftsmen and tradesmen — blacksmiths, wheelwrights, carpenters, millers, shoemakers and gardeners – and accounted for an increasing percentage of the male labour force, rising from 15% in 1841 to nearly 20% in 1871. Such large percentages are perhaps higher than might be expected in a rural parish and probably stem from the presence of the two large estates.

The other main sector of female employment in the parish was domestic service (excluding domestic servants in farming households). The proportion of women employed in this sector rose from around 20% in 1841 and 1851 to more than 35% in 1861 and to 45% in 1871. Even so, there are grounds to suggest that there may have been a measure of under-employment for the percentage of females over the age of 13 with no formal employment seems to have been rather high, running between 47% and 54% of women in this age group in the four censuses of the period, for not all the wives had small children to care for, nor was a significant proportion of the unmarried women too elderly to work. However one should not underestimate the informal employment available for women in a rural economy, not only in terms of work on farms at busy times of the year and casual domestic work for better-off neighbours, but cultivating the vegetable garden, feeding the house pig and fowls, gleaning at harvest time, and picking fruit and nuts and gathering stray wool on the commons.

The possibility of under-employment in the parish is also raised by the very few children under 13 in formal employment at a time when education was neither free nor compulsory: in 1841 one girl aged 12 was employed as a servant; in 1851 one girl aged 10 was employed as a house servant and a boy aged 12 was employed as a farm labourer; in 1861 two girls aged 11 and 12 were employed as servants; and in 1871 three boys aged 10, 11 and 12 were employed as farm labourers. It should not be assumed however that the other children aged between 5 and 12 attended school for the censuses show that only 51% of the 5-12 years age group were 'scholars' in 1851, 65% in 1861 and 80% in 1871. (Though the new school in the Terrace had not been completed by 1871, the latter figure indicates that the school was functioning in temporary premises elsewhere, see below.) Nor should it be assumed that all the scholars were regular attenders. At busy times of the farming year, such as lambing and harvest, education enjoyed a low priority on the part of farming and labouring households.

The restoration of St Andrew's, Norton[8]

The second half of the 19th century was a period of church restoration and rebuilding in Radnorshire, for 37 parish churches in the county were restored or rebuilt, much of the cost being borne by the local landed gentry. St Andrew's was the third of this rash of churches to be restored, even rebuilt, for as the *Hereford Times* of 12 September 1868 put it: 'The church has now the appearance of an entirely new erection rather than being a restoration.'

The restoration was much more extensive than was originally envisaged since the fabric of the church proved to have deteriorated to a much greater extent than had been thought. Much of the masonry, constructed of local stone, had weathered badly, while the old timber belfry, 'a very singular and quaint construction' according to the *Hereford Times*, was in need of renovation. The plans for the restoration were drawn up by the eminent architect Gilbert Scott, though he did not directly supervise the work, leaving this to his assistant James Burlinson. The task was not simply one of restoration but to fashion and adapt the church so that it reflected the aesthetic and liturgical ideals of the age, coloured by Richard Green Price's High Church views.

Plate 3: St Andrew's Church, Norton. (Courtesy of Joan Parker)

The pre-restoration building, long and low with a wooden belfry and no break in the roof line between nave and chancel – 'a curious looking Welsh church rather like a barn' according to Richard Green Price's daughter Laura[9] – was far removed from these ideals and from the concept of 'the beauty of holiness'. The interior walls, pulpit and screen were all white-washed, as were the exterior walls, judging from a photograph of the old church. In the nave box pews had been crammed in to maximise seating, while the western end was blocked up by the gallery erected by Sir Harford Jones Brydges in 1834. The chancel was separated from the nave by a low screen – renovated in 1868 and retained, though not to the taste of the *Hereford Times* correspondent who described it as 'dwarfish'.

The extension of the belfry cap into a spire and the addition of a vestry and north and south transepts transformed the external appearance of St Andrew's. The approach to the church was enhanced by a new boundary wall and lych-gate, the latter the gift of the builder, Mr Price of Presteigne. Inside the church, the removal of the gallery, the replacement of the old box pews – 'very moth eaten' according to Laura Meredith – by open seats, and the introduction of four large stained glass windows in the transepts and the east and west ends of the church gave the interior a greater sensation of spaciousness, while the new pulpit, lectern and tiled floor probably provided a hint of modernity, as did the organ by Forster and Andrews given by the Presteigne lawyer and banker, Cecil Parsons. Though the population of the parish had been increasing, the restoration had the perverse effect of reducing seating from the 208 claimed in the Religious Census of 1851 to 170.[10]

The cost of the restoration was £2,200. A church rate raised £400, the second baronet, Sir Harford James Jones Brydges gave £200, Richard Green Price gave a personal donation of £500 and his family and friends and the people of Norton contributed nearly £820, leaving an initial shortfall of rather more than £380.

Farming in Norton in the later 19th century

The pattern of landholding in the parish changed little in the second half of the century. The censuses of 1851-1901 showed the number of farms remaining stable at 17 or 18 until 1901 when the number fell to 16. However there was a measure of flexibility in the pattern, for while smaller holdings such as Holland's Lawn, Quarry, Townsend and Cook's House were usually merged with larger holdings, others such as Elvins and The Hazels, worked as a single unit in the 1840s and 1850s, became two separate holdings, and a new holding was created when 20 or so acres were attached to Norton Mill. At Boultibrooke and Norton Manor, farmland previously utilised as home farms worked by bailiffs was rented out to tenants in 1863 and 1867 respectively.[11] By the closing decades of the century Back Lane Farm had been split into two or three smaller holdings, while Impton Farm, whose land had been worked from Norton Manor since the days of Richard Price, reappeared, and the Norton Manor Home Farm, was worked briefly in the early 1880s by Frank Green Price.

However, there were significant changes in the pattern of landowning in the parish in the second half of the century when 705 acres of common land, mainly in the north of the parish, passed into private ownership as a result of the Enclosure Award of 1867.[12] The main beneficiary was Richard Green Price, who received 59 acres as lord of the manor and a further 479 acres in respect of the land he owned in the parish. The other beneficiaries were Edward Abley who received more than 35 acres in respect of his ownership of the Meeting House and Corns, Richard Edwards who received more than 54 acres in respect of the Meeting House and Bach farms, Arthur Partridge who gained rather more than 20 acres in respect of The Pools, Arthur Phillips slightly more than 21 acres in respect of The Hazels and Elvins and Sir Harford James Jones Brydges who received nearly 31 acres in respect of Boultibrooke estate lands in the parish.

The many straight field boundaries on Hawthorn Hill. Llanwen Hill and Stonewall Hill date from the years following the 1867 enclosure. The broadly rectangular fields, many with fairly straight boundaries, in the southern half of the parish between the village and Boultibrooke, were created over a longer time period and in a different manner as land-holders gradually consolidated their scattered quillets in each open field into larger blocks of land, either by exchange or purchase, in order to work their land more efficiently. Such a process may well have taken centuries to complete.

Name of farm	1845 acreage	1891 acreage
Blackpatch Farm	102	256
Carter's Farm	183	346
The Farm	186	223
Hill House	242	305
The Pools	53	63

Figure 22: Upland farms on the Norton Manor estate.
(Source Norton tithe schedule 1845 and Sale catalogue 1891)

A comparison of the acreages of some of the upland farms in the Norton Manor estate in 1845 and 1891 suggest that the lands gained by the enclosure award were used to increase the size of the upland farms on the estate. Green Price dominance of the parish was rein-forced by the purchase of Blackpatch Farm and the Pools at some point between 1867 and 1891.

The first half of the century provides few insights into land utilisation in the parish. In 1814 Arthur Phillips of The Hazels, a holding of 60 or so acres, found himself in financial difficulties and was forced to sell his stock, crops and implements and the advertisement in the *Hereford Journal* gives us a picture of his farming methods. His stock consisted of 4 cows and a heifer all in calf, 2 bullocks, 4 yearling heifers and 6 calves, 2 carthorses and a colt, and 300 sheep. He had 2 tons of hay in his barn and 5 acres of wheat, 2½ acres of barley, 3 acres of peas and 10 acres of oats. Phillips was therefore essentially a livestock farmer who made good use of the commons, judging from the size of his flock. Though he was to spend time in Presteigne Gaol in 1817 as a debtor, his family managed to remain owners not only of The Hazels, but also of Elvins.[13]

The tithe schedule of 1845 gives a fuller, though broader picture of land utilisation in the parish. Clearly livestock farming was dominant in the parish, for the arable acreage included not only cereals but also roots, clover and temporary leys.

In the last quarter of the 19th century British farming faced severe competition in its home market from cheaper farm products from the Americas and Australasia. The arable sector was the first to feel the pinch as cheap cereals began to flood in from the North American prairies in the 1870s, but in the 1880s the development of refrigeration enabled the beef producers of the Argentine pampas and the Australian grasslands, together with the sheep and dairy farmers of New Zealand, to target the British market. Between the 1870s and the 1890s wheat and wool prices fell by 50% and the livestock sector as a whole experienced falls of 25% in the same period.

Category	Acreage	%
Arable	670	22.7
Pasture	745	25.3
Meadow	363	12.3
Woodland	365	12.4
Common	807	27.3

Figure 23: Land utilisation in Norton, 1845

The crop and livestock returns for the parish suggest that impact of such changes upon local farming patterns was to reinforce the dominance of livestock farming, a trend aided, Dorothy Sylvester suggests, by the 1867 enclosure.[14] Thus the acreage under wheat fell from 16½% of the total arable acreage in the mid-1870s to 6½% in 1904-06, while over the same period the acreage under oats increased from about 17½% to more than 23% of the total arable acreage, reflecting its continuing importance as a feedstuff for livestock. The growing dominance of the livestock sector is demonstrated by the increase in the acreage under clover and rotational grass from 31% to 41% between the mid-1870s and 1904-06 and by the increase in permanent grassland by more than 28%, at the expense of rough pasture, in the same period.

The increase in the grassland acreage was not matched by an increase in the number of cattle or sheep kept – about 400 cattle and 3,000 sheep. However there is evidence to suggest a change in the age structure of the livestock kept, for the proportion of cattle under two years of age rose from 37% in the mid-1870s to 44% in 1904-06. This suggests that there was a growing tendency to market stock at under two years, rather than at two to three years, thus increasing farmers' cash flow. There is some evidence to suggest that the same trend may have been present in the sheep sector, for the proportion of lambs compared with wethers and ewes rose from 34% in the mid-1870s to 40% by 1904-06, though the trend was not consistent over the whole period. However it does suggest that the shift in consumers' taste from mutton to lamb may have begun by the opening years of the 20th century.

Despite some increase in cashflow, farm incomes fell in the closing decades of the 19th century, and Norton farmers were either unable or unwilling to increase stocking levels. Sir Harford James Jones Brydges sought to help his tenants by giving them rent rebates – 10% in April 1882.[15] Farmers also sought to cut costs by reducing the number of farm-workers they employed, hoping to maintain productivity by increasing mechanisation and employing casual labour at peak times of the year. Thus census data shows that whereas a total of 54 farm servants and farm labourers were employed in the parish in 1851, the number had fallen to 36 in 1891 and to 27 in 1901.

Norton in the later 19th century

The Agricultural Depression of the later 19th century initiated a decline in the population of the parish which was to continue well into the next century, a trend only briefly interrupted in 1901. The decline was most marked between 1871 and 1891 when the population fell by a quarter. The number of occupied houses in Norton also fell, though not so steeply.

	Population	Occupied houses
1871	357	66
1881	291	61
1891	266	58
1901	283	60

Figure 24: Norton population and housing, 1871-1901
(Source: Printed census data)

The sharp reduction in the number of farmworkers in the closing decades of the 19th century noted above was balanced by a marked increase in the number of female domestic servants other than on farms, the maximum coming in 1901 when 36 were so employed. The number of male domestic servants had also increased to 18, if gardeners are included in this category. This surge in domestic service seems to have come about through the 'gentrification' of the village as a result of Sir Richard's financial difficulties and his death in 1887 which led members of the family to settle in a suitable style in a number of other houses in the village, including at various times The Vicarage, The Gables built by Sir Richard after 1883 and probably intended to be used ultimately as a dower house, and Townsend Villa rebuilt and enlarged *c.*1895 by Sir Richard's son-in-law Powlett Milbank. In the meantime Milbank's wife Edith, the daughter of Sir Richard, had found it difficult to settle in Yorkshire and in 1892 Milbank purchased the Norton Manor estate from his

Plate 4: The Gables. (Courtesy George Lancett)

41

brother-in-law, the second baronet Sir Dansey Green Price, and returned to live in the Manor in a style befitting his wealth and station.

The Norton Manor establishment in 1901 consisted of a valet, two footmen, a hall boy, four grooms and a coachman, a housekeeper, three laundry maids, a still room maid, a schoolroom maid, a cook, four housemaids, two ladies' maids, a kitchen maid and a scullery maid. The three other gentry houses in the parish in 1901, Boultibrooke, the home of the widowed Lady Brydges, Townsend Villa now the home of the dowager Lady Green Price and her unmarried daughter Frances, and The Gables, the home of Whitmore Green Price, Sir Richard's youngest son, were staffed on a more modest scale.

6   NORTON MANOR IN THE 19TH CENTURY

As noted in the previous chapter, the Price family of Knighton, in the person of Richard Price I, had acquired Impton in 1766. Initially the Prices were non-resident, continuing to live at Knighton and staying at Impton on visits to Norton. Richard Price II, 1773-1861, lived at Impton in the opening years of the 19th century, according to W.H. Howse, returning to live at Chandos House in Knighton in 1807. When the house became the Chandos Arms in 1828 Price may have returned to Impton. However the *Hereford Journal* of 25 April 1838 announced

> On Friday 20 April the tenants and friends of R. Price assembled at the Chandos Arms to celebrate the laying of the first stone of the new mansion house Mr Price is erecting at Norton.

The house took some time to build since Richard Price was not in residence at the time of the 1841 census, which revealed plasterers, painters and masons as boarders at a number of houses in the village and probably still working on what was to become Norton Manor. This name implies that Price had acquired the lordship of Norton from the Harleys by the 1840s, but the precise date is far from clear. In one of his notebooks Howse suggests that it took place in 1814, the purchase, for £1,200, being completed by a Mr Davies, on behalf of Price. However the sale seems to have fallen through since Norton continued to be included in the list of Harley manors on which shooting game without permission was banned until 1829, when a licence was issued for the first time for Price's gamekeeper to protect the game on the manors of Bleddfa and Norton, which suggests that Price acquired the Norton lordship in that year.[1]

Educated at University College Oxford, he had been MP for Radnor Boroughs – Cefnllys, Knighton, Knucklas, New Radnor and Rhayader – since 1799, and was to continue to be until 1847, by which time he was Father of the House and in Radnorshire was known as 'Member' Price. He owed his electoral success not to any personal popularity, but to the fact that the Price family and the Lewis family of Harpton Court and their allies controlled four of the five boroughs which made up the constituency. Richard Price had been high sheriff of Radnorshire in 1794 and again briefly in 1799, and had served as lieutenant colonel of the Radnorshire Volunteers 1803-09 and then of the Radnorshire Local Militia.[2] A Conservative in politics – very much the 'stern unbending Tory' – he was a steadfast opponent of reform.

Richard Price was a bachelor and, rather reclusive and eccentric by the 1840s, probably more interested in trees than people; according to his great niece Laura he had a great dislike of children. Nor were her memories of Norton Manor at that time pleasing, 'the grey stoned gabled house' she thought gloomy and 'wanting many improvements', while the trees growing right up to the windows 'from the inside gave a dreary look to the place'.[3] Laura was aware that Price did not get on well with her father, his nephew Richard Green, who acted as Price's man of business, for he was initially a moderate Conservative, not unsympathetic to reform. Whereas

Plate 5: Richard Price of Norton Manor. (Courtesy The Judge's Lodgings, Presteigne)

Price wanted to keep the Corn Laws to protect the interests of landowners and arable farmers, Green believed that Free Trade was in the interests of the country as a whole.

On the death of Richard Price in 1861 his heir George Green, the oldest son of his sister Margaret, renounced his interest in the estate in favour of his younger brother Richard, who assumed the additional surname of Price by royal licence. After serving his articles in Worcester, Richard Green, with Thomas Peters, set up the successful legal practice of Green and Peters in Knighton. In 1836 Green went into banking, becoming a partner in the Kington, Knighton and Radnorshire Bank.

Even before he moved to Norton in 1861 Green Price was already one of the most influential figures in the county and increasingly seen as the coming man. He took a leading role in the transformation of Knighton into a modern forward-looking market town. He was instrumental in setting up the Temeside Agricultural Society and the Knighton Farmers' Club which did much to promote agricultural improvement in eastern Radnorshire.[4] His promotion of the Knighton and Central Wales railway line not only helped to confirm Knighton's status as the leading market town of the county and to develop Llandrindod Wells, but also raised his profile in the county as a whole. As county treasurer 1850-61 he had worked closely with the county establishment and was also an experienced local politician, having acted as the political agent for Frankland Lewis, Sir John Walsh and later for Sir George Cornewall Lewis of Harpton Court.

Richard Green's first marriage to Frances Dansey in 1837 was tragically short, and in 1844 he married Laura King. The 12 surviving children of the two marriages were commemorated by the planting of 12 *Wellingtonia Gigantea* at the southern approach to the village, an occasion recorded by an inscription on a stone on the site:

These timeless trees in this field (Wellingtonia Gigantea) were planted respectfully
by the twelve children of Sir Richard Green Price, Bt.
in the year 1865

Margaret Price = George Green of Ashford Hall, Shropshire
(1771-1827)

| George (1802-69) | Frances Dansey (1) = Richard = (2) Laura King (1803-87) | 2 sons | 3 daus |

| Richard Dansey (1838-1909) | Constance (1841-89) | Frances (1849-1942) | Milburga (1850-1939) | Edith (1851-1920) | Henrietta (1851-1937) | Laura (1853-1917) | Herbert Chase (Revd) (1855-1919) | Francis (1856-1885) | Alice (1859-1928) | Alfred (Revd) (1860-1940) | George Whitmore (1862-1939) |

| Dansey = (1864) Clara Dansey | Consty = (1865) Thomas Baskerville Mynors | Fanny | Milla = (1) (1871) Richard Dansey = (2) (1875) Powlett Milbank | | Netty = (1871) Arthur Tickell | Lily = (1881) Henry Meredith | Chase = (1895) Susan Barneby | Frank | = (1892) Edgar Moorsom | = (1893) Mary Edwards | = (1893) Rachel Burroughs |

Figure 25: The Green Price family
(Sources: Burke, Debrett and the notes of David Otterwill)

Over the years several of the trees have been badly damaged by gales and storms, while on 20 March 1977 a fireball or meteor truncated the eleventh tree.

On inheriting the estate Green Price realised that the Manor was too small to accommodate his large and growing family and during the early 1860s a new wing was added to the house. At the same time the gardens were laid out with terraces and croquet and archery lawns. He then turned his attention to the village itself, his first objective the provision of a vicarage to replace the old parsonage house, possibly the present Bircher Close. A substantial house with six main bedrooms, domestic quarters, a coach house and stabling was built to the north of St Andrew's in 1862. The new vicarage provided fitting accommodation for the Revd Benjamin Hill, inducted in 1860 and then living in the parsonage house, described by Green Price's daughter Laura as 'very old and dilapidated'.

When Green Price inherited the estate in 1861 he also secured the patronage of the living from the Crown. The drive he displayed in building the new vicarage and a few years later restoring the church suggest that he was following a coherent strategy of re-energising the Anglican cause in the parish. The previous vicar of the parish, the Revd John Jenkins, who was in post from 1827 until

Plate 6: Sir Richard Green Price.
(Courtesy The Judge's Lodgings, Presteigne)

1860 had been a pluralist holding the livings of both Knill and Norton and had chosen to live at Discoed. As noted in the previous chapter, by 1860 St Andrew's was in a deplorable state of repair.[5]

Green Price decided that Norton's school, described by Laura Green Price as 'very ugly in itself', which was maintained by Sir Harford Jones Brydges and which stood in the churchyard, should be relocated. At the re-opening of the restored church in 1868 he promised to provide a site and decided to set the school in the centre of a row of cottages he was building for his estate workers.[6] Number 4 The Terrace became both the house of the schoolmistress and the school itself, though when it began to function is not clear. There is no mention of a row of six cottages with a schoolmistress living in the centre in the 1871 census. It would therefore seem likely that the school began to operate in its new premises in late 1871 or early in 1872, although the large increase in the number of 'scholars' recorded in the 1871 census suggests that the new school may have been functioning at the time of the census in temporary premises such as the unused school building in the churchyard.

In her *Recollections* Laura Green Price rhapsodized over the remodelled Norton Manor:

> A lovely place and one to be proud of, and every day we grew fonder of it, with its lovely nooks and walks through the woods which we never tired of exploring.[6]

Plate 7: The Terrace.
(Courtesy of Joan Parker)

Plate 8: No. 4 The Terrace.
(Courtesy of Joan Parker)

Even so, the Green Price family spent much time away from their new home in the 1860s and early 1870s. In 1862-63 while the new wing and grounds were under construction they were on the Continent, while in 1869 the family took a three-year lease on a house in Cheltenham, while Richard Green Price, suffering from asthma, and his wife and their daughters Milburga and Edith spent the winter at Cannes. The family returned to the Manor for the summers of 1871 and 1872, but it was not until 1873 that they took up permanent residence.[7]

The presence of a large, young and lively family at the Manor, rather than the reclusive and somewhat intimidating Richard Price, seems to have been welcomed in the village. According to Laura Green Price, the family's arrival in 1861 was greeted by the ringing of the church bells and the roadside lined with well-wishers who cheered them heartily as they passed on their way to their new home. The relationship between the Green Prices and the people of Knighton, Norton and Presteigne seems to have been harmonious. On the marriages of Milburga in 1871, Edith in 1875 and Laura in 1881, all at the parish church, the brides received generous wedding presents from all three places. The local people joined in the celebrations, funded in the case of Knighton and Presteigne by the local tradesmen, while in Norton the family seems to have organised the public tea and sports. To some measure all parties – Green Price, his tenants and workmen and the tradesmen of the two towns – were motivated by self-interest: Green Price by a desire to maintain his reputation as a paternalistic and benevolent landlord; the others by a desire to protect their livelihoods. Popular goodwill nevertheless seems to have been sincere: in 1875 a crowd of more than 4,000 gathered at Knighton railway station to see off Edith and her husband Powlett Milbank on their honeymoon, as did 'thousands' when Laura and her husband Henry Meredith set off on their honeymoon in 1881 from the same station.[8]

Most social events in the district were attended by Green Price – created a baronet in 1874 – sometimes accompanied by his wife, though occasionally his oldest son Dansey

Plate 9: Norton Manor. (Courtesy the late Cherry Leversedge)

represented the family. As convention dictated, the Green Price girls, all educated at home, kept out of the public eye. However Henrietta and then Laura served as organist and choirmistress at St Andrew's, while Edith, an accomplished horsewoman, enjoyed hunting. For the most part their social life revolved around visits to and from relatives and neighbouring gentry families such as the Evelyns of Corton.

The Green Price boys attended public schools such as Eton, Cheltenham and Repton and thus were away from the district for most of the year. Even so, the family made a major contribution to the sporting life of the locality. Sir Richard and his son Dansey were greatly interested in horse breeding, racing and fox hunting, while his other sons were patrons of the Presteigne Archery Club of the 1860s, the Polo Club of 1874 and later of the Golf Club formed in 1897 which had its first course at Paradise. The family provided two members of the Presteigne football team which defeated Leominster Scarlet Runners 5-1 in 1880. Members of the family played cricket for the Radnorshire and then the Gentlemen of Radnorshire XIs and, through their public school connections, were able to ensure the success of the Knighton Cricket Week by arranging matches with first class teams such as MCC Club and Ground and I Zingari. Family connections with local cricket continued into the 1920s when the third baronet, Sir Robert Green Price, played for Knighton and his uncle, the Revd Alfred Green Price, turned out for Presteigne.

Green Price owned relatively little property in Presteigne and showed great tact and sensitivity in his dealings with the town, for the Jones Brydges of Boultibrooke claimed lordship over part of it. Thus, after taking a leading part in the building of the Market Hall and Assembly Rooms in Presteigne, he ensured that it was Lady Brydges who laid the foundation stone of the building in September 1865. With the building of the Presteigne railway line it was a different matter: Sir Richard and his son Dansey had provided most of the funds to build the line and it was Sir Richard's daughter Edith, deputising for her mother, who inaugurated the line by cutting the first sod in 1872.[9] In Norton however, Green Price was lord of the manor and by far the largest landowner and thus the initiative lay with him in such matters as the restoration of the church and the enclosure of commons and waste.

Whereas Green Price, as lord of the manor, concerned himself, in the main, with Norton, Jones Brydges saw his Boultibrooke estate as part of the wider Presteigne locality, where he claimed the lordship of the mesne manor. The differing priorities of Norton Manor and Boultibrooke can be seen in the local celebrations of the wedding of the Prince of Wales and Princess Alexandra of Denmark in 1863. At Norton Manor the 60 tenants and men working on the estate were provided with dinner while the female staff, and the estate wives and children were provided with tea and plum pudding. Mrs Green Price also presented each child with a medal. The celebrations concluded with the lighting of two bonfires, one below and one above the Manor. At Boultibrooke the celebrations were in part Presteigne based. The men of the estate were given dinner at the Sun Inn in the town while Lady Brydges entertained the female staff, wives and children to tea at Boultibrooke House. Bonfires were lit at both Presteigne and Boultibrooke, while Jones Brydges took the chair at the celebratory dinner for the local elite at the Radnorshire Arms in Presteigne.[10]

Sir Richard's interests as a landowner extended far beyond Norton, for more than more than half of the Green Price estate lay outside the parish. In addition he had a prosperous legal practice in Knighton until the later 1860s. With his son Dansey he was involved in developing the up and coming spa town of Llandrindod Wells, founded upon the enclosure of the local commons and the arrival of the Central Railway railway line en route for Builth and Llandovery, the latter being reached in 1868.

Enclosure and railway development were two of Sir Richard's major enthusiasms. The former is understandable since a large estate owner gained significantly from the enclosure of commons and waste, particularly if he was lord of the manor. There was also always the possibility that parts of the common sold to defray expenses could be purchased relatively cheaply. Thus Richard Price and Richard Green Price were involved in nine enclosures in the county in which they were allotted 3,500 acres of commons, nearly doubling the acreage of the family estate.[11]

The enthusiasm of Sir Richard for railway development was completely uncritical. He invested heavily in all three phases of the Central Wales line, on occasions mortgaging his estates in order to advance money to enable construction to proceed, accepting in payment shares which in the long run proved to be worthless. Without Sir Richard's financial backing neither the Presteigne line connecting with the Leominster-Kington line at Titley, nor the extension of the line from Kington to New Radnor, both opened in 1875, would have been built.[12] Since Dansey Green Price shared his father's enthusiasm for railway building, the impact upon family finances was disastrous and the mortgages on the estate were not completely redeemed until 1960.

The return of Richard Green Price unopposed as MP for the Radnor Boroughs on the sudden and unexpected death of Sir George Cornewall Lewis, the sitting Member, in 1863 was not surprising, given his high profile and the backing he received from the establishment in the constituency, for the seat was virtually a Lewis/Price pocket borough. The same factors help to account for his return unopposed in 1863 and 1868, though the unqualified backing he gave to the Liberals and their leader W.E. Gladstone in 1868 suggests that party politics played a larger role than was the norm in Radnorshire elections.

In January 1869 Green Price resigned his seat to enable the Marquis of Hartington to contest it in a by-election, in order that he could join Gladstone's cabinet. This move was clearly more in the interests of the Liberal Party rather than in the interests of the local electorate and raised suspicion as to Green Price's motives. Thus at the declaration of the poll in Hartington's favour there was a shout of 'Who sold the Boroughs?', a charge that was to haunt Green Price for the rest of his life, particularly after he was made a baronet in the Dissolution honours of 1874.

Thus when he contested the Radnorshire County seat in 1874 and 1880 he was taunted with:

> There was an MP came from Norton,
> His stay in the House was a short 'un,
> For as I am told,
> Radnor Boroughs he sold,
> And the Marquis of Hartington bought 'em.[13]

Unsuccessful in 1874, he won the Radnorshire seat in 1880, but his second spell in Parliament was not a happy one. He was dogged by financial difficulties as a result of the agricultural depression, his heavy investment in local railways and the need to provide for his large family on a scale befitting their social status. Moreover his health, never robust, was deteriorating as a result of old age – he was 77 in 1880 – and health problems necessitated long absences from the House. It led some in Radnorshire to wonder

> As to whether Sir Richard was the representative of the County in the House of Commons, or a representative of the House of Commons in Radnorshire.[14]

By this time he could no longer afford to live at the Manor which was let on a seven-year lease, and in 1883 he and Lady Green Price and their two unmarried daughters moved into Norton Vicarage to live with their son Chase Green Price, now curate in the parish. The move and the death of his son Francis in an accident in a steeplechase in 1885 at Brecon hit him badly. In the Radnorshire election of 1885 he was defeated decisively, largely as a result of his wholehearted support of Gladstone's policy of Home Rule for Ireland and his increasingly radical home policy.[15] He never returned to Norton Manor and died in London on 11 August 1887 after a short illness and two unsuccessful operations.

A memorial to Sir Richard was subsequently erected on Hawthorn Hill, but this might seem superfluous since few have had such a profound impact upon their wider local environment as he has had. The Knighton townscape still bears his imprint in the form of the railway station, the sheep market, now a car park, and the Knighton Hotel, as do Llandrindod Wells and Norton. In Presteigne, with the closing of the railway in 1964, only the renovated Market Hall and Assembly Room remain as a memorial to him, while the closure of the Kington-New Radnor line have all but removed evidence of his achievements in those towns. Possibly the Central Wales line, perhaps the most striking symbol of his drive and determination, is his most appropriate memorial.

Plate 10: The monument commemorating the life and achievements of Sir Richard Green Price

7   Boultibrooke in the 19th Century

For the greater part of the century Boultibrooke was owned by the Jones Brydges family, descendants of the Jones family of Trewern who, along with the Lewis family of Harpton Court and the Price family of Monaughty, had played a prominent role in Radnorshire during the 16th and early 17th centuries. The family suffered heavy financial losses during the Civil War period through their support for the Crown, but its status was restored by Captain (later Colonel) James Jones who had distinguished himself at the battle of Blenheim in 1704, receiving a sword of honour from Queen Anne. The family fortunes were greatly enhanced by his third marriage in 1706 to Mary, the daughter of Bridgestock Harford, by which he gained an interest in the extensive Harford estates in south and west Herefordshire. The son of this marriage, Harford Jones, married Elizabeth, the daughter of the wealthy William Brydges of Bosbury, who brought with her as her dowry the Whittern estate at Lyonshall.

The Radnorshire home of the couple was at Walton Hall and they subsequently acquired Harford House in Hereford Street, Presteigne as their town house. By 1774 the status of the family was sufficient for Harford Jones, or his son, Harford Jones II to be included amongst those considered for appointment as high sheriff of Radnorshire. Harford Jones

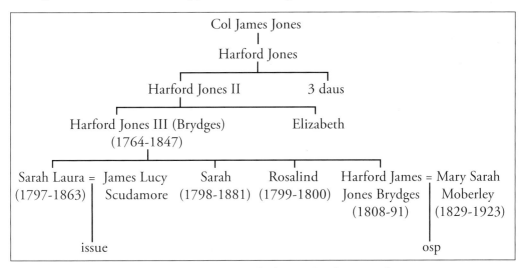

Figure 26: A concise Harford Jones Brydges genealogy.
(Source: Kentchurch Court Papers, Hereford County Record Office)

II married Winifred, the daughter of the wealthy Richard Hooper of Kington and the marriage produced two children, Harford Jones III, (who took the additional surname of Brydges in 1826, in accordance with the will of his maternal grandmother) and Elizabeth who died unmarried *c.*1792.[1]

Harford Jones III entered the service of the East India Company as a cadet, serving in Basra in present-day Iraq, first as an assistant and then as factor. He gained a reputation as a gifted linguist and developed a strong interest in the culture and history of Persia. In 1798 he became the company's resident at Baghdad, serving there until 1806. In 1807 he was created a baronet and appointed as envoy to the court of the Shah of Persia at Tehran, charged with blocking Russian and French attempts to curb British dominance in India. The negotiations leading to the treaty of 1809 which

Plate 11: Portrait of Sir Harford Jones Brydges by Sir Thomas Lawrence

effectively blocked France from the route to India were, according to Dr M.E. Yapp, in his *Strategies of British India, Iran and Afghanistan*, 'rude and colourful'. Thus, when a Persian minister implied that Harford Jones was cheating, Jones called him 'a stupid old blockhead', threatened to knock him down, and rampaged around the tent, knocking over the furniture and fittings. On his return from Persia in 1811, disappointed by his failure to rise as high in the East India Company as he thought he deserved, Harford Jones resigned. If disillusioned with the company, he remained fascinated by Persian culture and history, publishing a number of books on the subject in the 1830s.[2]

In 1812 Sir Harford purchased the Boultibrooke estate and promptly began to remodel the house to bring it up to a standard fitting for Radnorshire's only resident baronet. The most striking addition was the library, a single storey extended octagonal building, designed by Robert Smirke to house Sir Harford's extensive collection of books and manuscripts on Persia. Sir Harford took great pride in laying out his gardens, greenhouses, hothouses, woodlands and ornamental pleasure grounds in a manner which attracted favourable public comment.[3]

Boultibrooke, which had its own laundry and corn mill, employed a large labour force of domestic staff, gardeners, farm labourers and estate workers, functioned as an autonomous community, almost independently of Norton and Presteigne. Sir Harford had a highly paternalistic regard for his employees who continued to receive full wages long after ill health or age prevented them from doing a full day's work, and when they retired, a small pension. At Christmas his workmen and pensioners were entertained to a meal of roast beef and plum pudding at one of Presteigne's inns, while Lady Brydges entertained

Plate 12: Boultibrooke. (Courtesy of the late Cherry Leversedge)

female employees and pensioners to tea at Boultibrooke. His benevolence also extended to the wider local community. He maintained a small school in Norton churchyard for the children of Norton and in 1834 he paid for the erection of a gallery in Norton church, on condition that three rows of sittings in it were reserved for his servants. The poor and aged of Norton and Presteigne also received gifts of warm clothing and sometimes food or coal from Boultibrooke at Christmas.

As befitted his rank, he was appointed as a Justice of the Peace on taking up residence and in 1816 served as high sheriff of Radnorshire. Between 1818 and 1822 he served as chairman of the Bench, and under his leadership the decision was taken to condemn the county's civic buildings, the Shire Hall on the corner of Presteigne's High Street and Broad Street and the county gaol on Broad Street, both in a dilapidated state, and to rebuild on new sites. The new gaol was built on the site now occupied by John Beddoes School by 1821, but the building of the new Shire Hall on the site of the old gaol in Broad Street did not begin until the later 1820s.[4]

Sir Harford's standing in Presteigne was not always as great as he would have wished. His attempts to buy the manor and borough of Presteigne from the Crown in 1817 and 1827 came to nothing, while his fussy attempts to exercise his authority in his so-called mesne manor of Presteigne alienated some of the townspeople.[5] However his support for parliamentary reform in the early 1830s brought him great popularity and the *Hereford Times* of 28 November 1831 contained a notice signed by the bailiff of Presteigne and 126 townsmen thanking him for the 'able and unflinching support he has given to the cause of Reform'. His advocacy of reform also brought him a measure of public recognition, though not the peerage some thought he coveted, for in 1831 Oxford University gave him an honorary DCL and in 1832 he was appointed a privy councillor.

Sir Harford's last political triumph came in 1835 when the Grey Coat Club, a Liberal electoral organisation which he had helped to form during the campaign for parliamentary reform, was largely responsible for the victory of the Whig Walter Wilkins over the Tory Sir John Walsh in the Radnorshire parliamentary election. In the 1840s, with his health declining, he retired into private life and died in March 1847 at the age of 83.

Dr Yapp maintained that Sir Harford's achievements in Baghdad and Tehran were under-estimated, not only at the time, but also subsequently.[6] His later local achievements have likewise never received due recognition from local historians, notably the renewal of the county's civic buildings in Presteigne and his championship of parliamentary reform. Such underestimation stems largely from his complex personality and temperament. Dr Yapp sees him as having a violent temper, prone to quarrel with associates, and always prepared to intrigue and deceive in order to achieve his objective. In Radnorshire his tendency to stand on his dignity and his readiness to take deep offence at any perceived slight led to a deep personal antipathy between him and Thomas Frankland Lewis of Harpton Court which embarrassed the county establishment.

In part this mutual hostility stemmed from political differences for Lewis was a Conservative whose attitude to parliamentary reform was ambiguous. Jones Brydges had opposed the election of Lewis as MP for Radnorshire in 1828 and in the reform campaign of 1831-32 developed the habit of denouncing Lewis at public political meetings and then leaving before Lewis or one of his allies had chance to reply.[7]

There were also personal differences between the two. Jones Brydges was a substantial landowner in the borough of New Radnor but was consistently denied any public appoint-ment in its administration. He attributed this to hostility on the part of Frankland Lewis, refusing to accept the assurance of Lewis that only those resident in the borough were eligible for public office.[8] Frankland Lewis on the other hand regarded Jones Brydges as a 'nabob' and 'new money', despite his impressive lineage, and enjoyed teasing him on his failure to secure a peerage.

Sir Harford's quarrelsome nature made it difficult for his fellow reformers to work with him, but the major factor here was that Sir Harford was an old fashioned Whig who believed that the Reform Act of 1832 was the culmination of a process which had begun with the Glorious Revolution of 1688-89, whereas his allies saw the Act as a beginning of the widening of the franchise which would lead ultimately to a true democracy.

Sir Harford James Jones Brydges

The second baronet had been educated at Merton College, Oxford and had been prevented from pursuing a naval career by ill health. Instead he travelled extensively in Europe and North America and built up a large natural history collection that presumably included *lepidoptera*, stuffed animals, birds and birds' eggs. It was on his travels that Jones Brydges met and married Mary Sarah Moberly in Nova Scotia, Canada in 1851. Born in Yorkshire in 1829, she was the oldest of nine children of Captain John Moberly RN and his wife Mary, the daughter of General Fock, who had commanded the Russian Imperial Artillery in the Battle of Borodino in 1812. The Moberly family, who had founded an Anglo-Russian banking house in St Petersburg, claimed descent from Robert Cozens, an illegitimate son of

Czar Peter the Great. Captain Moberly and his family settled in Canada in the mid-1830s and the new Lady Jones Brydges probably had enjoyed a less socially restricted upbringing than that of her British contemporaries.[9]

The second baronet and his wife seem to have been popular not only in Norton but also in Presteigne. For example, when the couple returned from a five-month visit to Canada in October 1857 they were greeted by a crowd of well-wishers and Presteigne town band, which returned the following day for a short extempore concert, while the church bells in Presteigne also celebrated their safe homecoming.[10]

Like his father, the second baronet took his responsibilities to his tenants, employees and dependants seriously: tenants received rent rebates in difficult years, workers were entertained at Christmas and employees unable to work were given small pensions. During long spells of snow or hard weather when labourers were unable to find work, such as in December 1853, a kitchen was set up in the courtyard of Boultibrooke to provide soup and bread for needy families and the elderly of the locality.[11]

From the 1860s it seems to have been tacitly accepted that primacy in Norton lay with the (Green) Price family in their capacity at lords of the manor and Jones Brydges looked increasingly to Presteigne as his sphere of influence, though he maintained the school in Norton churchyard until 1871. In 1854 Jones Brydges headed the subscription list to fund the restoration of Presteigne parish church, and later provided land for the cemetery. However his dogged championship of Presteigne's status as the premier town of Radnorshire met with little success: in the 1870s he opposed the dissolution of Presteigne Poor Law Union, the withdrawal of the Radnorshire Militia headquarters from Presteigne to Brecon and the closure of the county gaol, all to no avail, while in 1889 Radnorshire County Council moved its headquarters from Presteigne to Llandrindod Wells.[12]

The second baronet and his wife, who preferred to be known as Lady Brydges, had a genuine enthusiasm for improving educational opportunities in the locality. In 1855 Lady Brydges established a Ragged School in Presteigne to provide a free education for those children whose parents were unable or unwilling to pay the fees charged by the other schools in the town. In 1865 she built the 'Iron School' on Mill Lane with Mrs Weatherstone, the wife of Boultibrooke's head gardener, as the teacher. It was a mixed school which could take 60 pupils and, after the National School had opened in Presteigne in 1870, it functioned as an infant school until it closed in 1892. The Jones Brydges also played a leading part in the building of the Presteigne National School: Sir Harford chaired the committee responsible for establishing the school and also gave land adjoining the Knighton road as its site.[13]

The second baronet continued the strong horticultural tradition at Boultibrooke. In the grounds, which extended to the bank of the Lugg opposite St Mary's Mill, summerhouses and gazebos were built and the shrubberies and gardens remodelled in accordance with current horticultural fashion. Given Jones Brydges' deep loathing of non-conformists, it is difficult to explain the good relationship which clearly existed between him and Mr Weatherstone, Boultibrooke's head gardener, a leading light of Presteigne's Baptist Chapel and of the town's teetotallers.[14]

Lady Brydges fulfilled those roles expected of a lady of rank, taking her turn to act as patroness of important social events such as the County Ball at Presteigne Assembly

Plate 13: The gardens at Boultibrooke c.1920. (Courtesy of George Lancett)

Rooms and the Invitation Ball, the most important function in Knighton's social calendar. However, her social horizons extended far beyond her class. She was a leading figure in Presteigne Horticultural Society which functioned intermittently in the 1850s, 1860s and later 1880s and whose show was often held at Boultibrooke. On such occasions she made a point of inviting the pupils of her two Presteigne schools to attend although they were not children of parents at home in polite society.[15] In 1898 the society was revived in a new form when Presteigne Oddfellows decided to celebrate their anniversary on August Bank Holiday Monday and to hold a floral fete and athletics sports at Boultibrooke by invitation of the then widowed Lady Brydges. This established a precedent and until the outbreak of the First World War the August Bank Holiday Monday Show at Boultibrooke was a landmark event in the social life of the Presteigne locality.

She also played a prominent role in the musical life of Presteigne. She was an active member of the Philharmonic Society of the 1860s and early 1870s, not only attending the concerts but also performing in them, sometimes with her younger sister and her brother, for the Moberlys seem to have been gifted musicians, playing the piano and the violin. In the Philharmonic Society she worked with 'Professor' Blackmore, Presteigne's professional musician, who had come to the town in 1854 as the Bugle Major of the Radnorshire Militia. In the 1860s and 1870s he was the bandmaster of the Presteigne Company of the Radnorshire Volunteers and also conducted a quadrille band which played at local dances. He also acted as choirmaster at the Primitive Methodist and Baptist chapels and also at the parish church, in addition to giving piano and singing lessons. Even so he barely scraped a living and an important source of income was his annual benefit concert. Lady Brydges took part, with other members of the Philharmonic Society, in at least one such concert.

Plate 14: A view of Norton c.1920. (Courtesy of George Lancett)

In the 1860s women of the gentry class were expected to lead their lives out of the public gaze except in connection with their charitable work, and Lady Brydges' playing at concerts which also featured professional performers may well have created a stir in local circles.[16] Blackmore certainly had little in common with the Jones Brydges beyond a love of music, for he was a Radical in politics, a Methodist local preacher and an enthusiastic teetotaller, whose sons in the early 1870s were officers in the Presteigne branch of the West of England Agricultural Labourers Association.[17]

In accordance with Sir Harford Brydges' will, on his death in 1891 the Boultibrooke estate passed to Lady Brydges for the duration of her life. In 1898 she gave a meadow at the rear of Presteigne County School to provide a sports field for the new secondary school. She also played a leading part in the campaign to secure places for girls and in 1902 was one of the guarantors of the monies raised to carry out the necessary alterations. The first girls, 12 in all, were admitted in September 1902.[18]

Lady Brydges was also instrumental in securing a modern water supply for Presteigne. In 1901 a scheme had been devised which envisaged lifting water from New Mill in Mill Lane and pumping it to a reservoir just below the Warden above the National School (a primary school) and then piping it to the town by gravitation. Lady Brydges enabled the scheme to be implemented in 1903, by agreeing to give a 25-year lease of the New Mill to the newly formed Presteigne Water Company, along with rights to a spring in Colebrook Meadow and a well in New Mill Orchard, and by allowing the water to be conveyed over her land to the reservoir below the Warden.[19]

On Lady Brydges' death on 1 October 1923 the estate passed to the representatives of the late Colonel Edward Lucas Scudamore of Kentchurch, a great nephew of her husband who had died in 1917. Lady Brydges' obituary in *The Times* of 9 October concluded: 'Her kindness and generosity to all she knew was proverbial.' But gracious as this tribute was, it does not tell the whole truth, for she seems to have been able to step across both the class and generational divides with ease, probably because she had grown up in a less rigid and inhibited environment than that normally associated with young women of the British upper class. Thus in 1901, at the age of 72 she was the first named patron of an invitation dance organised to raise funds for St Andrew's Football Club, not the type of social function with which she was familiar. Even so, one would be surprised if she had not managed the occasion with considerable aplomb.[20]

8   NORTON IN THE 20TH CENTURY

For much of the first half of the century elements of continuity obscured the radical changes which were taking place in the character of the parish; socially it remained dominated by the gentry, despite the breakup of the two large estates, while the pattern of landholding remained much as it had been in the 19th century. Again the local economy continued to spiral downwards as, apart from the war years of 1914-18 and 1939-45 and the post-Second World War years, farming continued to experience difficulties.

Population and housing

The steady fall in population in the parish reflects not only the shedding of labour by farmers as they sought to cut costs and the reduction in domestic staff at the two big houses during the inter-war years, but also 'pull factors' such as the better housing and social amenities, together with greater job opportunities and higher wages, in the service sector in the towns and cities.

	Population	Occupied houses
1901	283	60
1911	271	67
1921	261	56
1931	230	55
1951	210	63

Figure 27: Population and housing
in Norton 1901-51.
(Source: printed census data)

Landholders and landowners

The pattern of landholding at the beginning of the 20th century showed little change from that of the previous half century. Thus the number of holdings remained at 18 or 19, while the variation in size of the holdings closely resembled that of 1845. However the pattern of landowning in the parish was transformed in the 1920s with the sale first of the Norton Manor estate and then of the Boultibrooke estate. Prior to the 1920s Norton had been dominated by these two large estates but after they had been sold, the farms and smallholdings in the parish were, for the most part, owner-occupied.

Acreage	No. of holdings, 1845	No. of holdings 1925
Under 20 acres	5	4
20 -99 acres	4	5
100 acres+	10	10

Figure 28: Size of holdings in Norton in 1845 and 1925
(Sources: 1845 tithe schedule and crop and livestock return, 1925)

On the death of Sir Richard Green Price in 1887 the Norton Manor estate, along with the other Green Price estates and property, passed to his son Sir Dansey Green Price. His financial plight seems to have been greater than that of his father, and after selling mainly commercial properties in Knighton in 1891, he sold the Norton Manor estate in 1892 to his brother-in-law, Powlett Milbank, who inherited his father's baronetcy in 1898.

Sir Powlett, who served as MP for Radnorshire between 1895 and 1900, and as Lord Lieutenant of the county from 1895 until his death in 1918, ran the estate on traditional paternalistic lines. Thus at the celebrations of his silver wedding anniversary in July 1900, the tenants of the estate and other residents of Norton were entertained to dinner in a marquee on the lawn of the Manor and presented Sir Powlett and Lady Edith with two silver candlesticks, a silver shoe horn and a silver button hook.[1]

However his son, Sir Frederick Milbank, had few ties in the county after his mother had died in 1903 and in 1919 he put the Norton Manor estate up for sale, preferring to settle on

Plate 15: Sir Powlett Milbank. (Courtesy of The Judge's Lodgings, Presteigne)

his Yorkshire estates.[2] The estate was purchased by Major A. Lindsey Careless, a member of the well-known legal family based in Llandrindod. Only a few years later, in 1923, Careless decided to sell nearly all the estate, placing the valuation, pricing and management of the sale in the hands of the much respected J.R. Bache of Knighton. The prices he fixed for the individual properties were considered 'extremely reasonable' by the *Radnor Express* of 20 March.

The properties were offered for sale in two tranches. The first, in mid-February, included Home Farm, Norton Mill Farm, Hares Green Farm, The Farm, Taylor's Farm, the Pools and the Post Office; the second, towards the end of September, included Hill House Farm, Old Impton, Blackpatch and Elvins, together with 470 acres of accommodation land on Hawthorn Hill.[3] Not all the properties were sold at the two auctions, some failing to reach the reserve price, while others were withdrawn from sale before the auction to be sold privately later. The problem was not the low level of prices, but the reluctance of many prospective purchasers, most of them existing tenants, to take part in a public auction because they believed the price they paid to be a private rather than a public matter and/or because they believed that privately they could negotiate a better price.

The breakup of the Boultibrooke estate was heralded by the announcement in the *Radnor Express* of 25 February 1926 that Mrs E. Lucas Scudamore was offering for sale outlying parts of the estate in Presteigne, Kington and Lyonshall, amounting to 764 acres in all and including Whitewall, Dolley and Ackhill Farms. In the end the two latter farms were withdrawn, but a trend had begun which, in a few years, led to the sale of all the farmland and ultimately of Boultibrooke House itself.

The break-up of the two large estates began the transformation of the pattern of landownership in Norton, for whereas in 1895 90% of arable and grassland had been rented, by 1985 90% was owner-occupied with the bulk of the change coming in the 1920s.[4] Norton was not unique, for at that time large landed estates were faring badly as a result of heavy taxation on high incomes imposed by Lloyd George in the 1910 budget, the inflationary pressures of the war years and the slump of the inter-war years. Some estates, such as the Penybont estate (1926) and the Clungunford estate (1931) were sold in their entirety, but more frequently a part of the estate, often tactfully described as 'an outlying part', was sold to ease financial pressures. This was the action taken at Harpton Court and the Green Price settled estate in 1920, and at Stanage Park in 1930.[5] The Norton Manor and Boultibrooke estate sales fall in this latter category for they were outliers of the Milbanks' Yorkshire and the Scudamores' Kentchurch estates respectively.

Farming in Norton in the first half of the 20th century

The two world wars had an impact on farming, changing cropping and stocking patterns drastically. Any conclusions from an analysis of the crop and livestock returns for the years 1905, 1915, 1925, 1935 and 1945 are thus of necessity tentative and very broad. During the decades of peacetime the arable acreage remained stable, but in the wartime years of 1915 and 1945 it increased substantially, as the result of marked increases in the acreage of rotational grass in those years. Of cereal crops, oats continued to occupy the largest acreage, between 27% and 33% of the arable acreage, the exception being 1915 when it comprised 15%. During peacetime the acreage of permanent grass tended to increase steadily at the expense of rough grazing, but in 1915 and 1945 it had fallen back sharply.

As far as livestock are concerned, while the number of sheep and cattle in the parish tended to rise between 1905 and 1935, by 1945 stocking levels had fallen back. The proportion of cattle under 2 years old had risen from 30% of the herd in 1905 to between 40 and 50% plus in later years, but surprisingly, the proportion of lambs in the flock in 1945 had only risen a few percentage points from the 40% of 1905. While Herefords remained the dominant breed of cattle, the Shropshire Down breed of sheep, dominant in the locality during the second half of the 19th century, had been completely displaced by the Kerry Hill and Clun Forest breeds in the inter-war years.

Productivity had risen significantly however. In 1901 the male labour force had totalled 51, but by 1935 it consisted of 21 full time males and 4 part-timers, while in 1945, despite the drive to increase food production, the labour force consisted of 20 full time males, 4 part-timers and 6 prisoners of war.[6] To some extent the productivity increase was attributable to increased mechanisation, for the number of horses employed in agriculture fell by a third between 1905 and 1935, while during the Second World War the 'War Ag' – the War Agricultural Executive Committee – spared no efforts to encourage mechanisation.

At first sight women appear to have made little contribution on the farm in the interwar years, for the 1935 crop and livestock returns for Norton show the female labour force as no more than three full-time and two part-time workers. However this statistic is misleading since it ignores the unpaid work of the wives and daughters of most farmers – in the garden, in the dairy making cream and butter, looking after the chickens, and, after a pig had been killed, salting bacon, curing ham, making brawn, faggots and pork pies, cooking the tongue and so putting the whole of the carcass to good use. The products were kept for use at home, sold to customers in the village or at Presteigne market on Wednesdays or at Knighton market on Thursdays – and all this done in addition to the housework and without any 'mod cons'! The income produced by their efforts was far from insignificant.

The survival off the old order

For most of the first half of the century the people of Norton were apparently content to leave the administration of the parish in the hands of the local gentry. In 1894 the rate-payers were offered the opportunity to elect a parish council, but rejected the idea by 13 votes to 5, instead voting in Powlett Milbank as chairman of the parish meeting which was to be held at least once a year. When he resigned in 1896, he was succeeded by his brother-in-law Whitmore Green Price, who served as chairman until 1933 when he was replaced by his brother, the Reverend Alfred Green Price, who served until 1939.[7]

Boultibrooke also played its part. Lady Brydges served as manager of Norton School from 1903 until 1919, when she received a vote of thanks for 'the unfailing interest she showed in everything appertaining to the welfare of education in the parish'. Almost inevitably she was succeeded as manager of the school by Mrs Whitmore Green Price who served until 1925 when she resigned on grounds of ill health and was replaced by the Reverend Green Price.[8]

After the sale of Boultibrooke House, the new owners also enjoyed considerable status in Norton. From the early 1930s until the mid-1950s the owner was Mr Loftus Otway Clarke (1876-1954), formerly of the Indian Civil Service, who had served as assistant commissioner of Assam and as a district magistrate in West Bengal, and who served as high sheriff of Radnorshire in 1939. He shared the house with a Major Johnson Atkinson Busfeild (1877-1960) and his wife, Marion Sarah, who was the sister of Clarke. Major Busfeild had had a good war: in November 1914 when only a captain he had briefly commanded the 1st Battalion of the Cheshire Regiment during the first battle of Ypres, being mentioned in dispatches, and later was awarded the DSO. On the resignation of the Reverend Alfred Green Price as manager of Norton School in 1937, he was succeeded by Major Busfeild who, in 1940, was elected chairman of the parish meeting, though it is not clear how long he served in this capacity.[9]

With Alfred Green Price as the incumbent between 1925 and 1939, Whitmore Green Price at The Gables until 1939 and Frances Green Price at Townsend until her death in 1942, some in the parish may have felt that time had stood still in Norton. Even after the sale of the Manor, the family enjoyed a high status in the locality for the third baronet, Sir Robert Green Price, was a major landowner in the county and served as high sheriff in 1930. That feeling of continuity seems to have extended beyond Norton, for as Eddie Taylor explained in the W.I.'s *Memories of Norton*, while Alfred Green Price was the incumbent, many establishment figures living near Norton – Lord Rennell of Rodd, Mrs Lee of Silia, Brigadier-General and Mrs Prescott Decie of Combe House, Mr and Mrs Robert

Thompson of Green End House, Mr and Mrs Newall of Corton and Dr Walker of Warden Court – were regular attenders at Sunday morning service at St Andrew's, all possibly nostalgic for 'the good old days'.

In general the people of the parish were prepared to let the big houses in Norton take the initiative, but on one issue, that of disestablishing the Anglican Church in Wales so that it ceased to be the official Church of the country, the views of the local elite, largely English in outlook, eventually diverged from those of many in the parish. Initially many opposed the idea of disestablishing the Anglican Church in Wales and in the summer of 1912 a petition against such a step was signed by 103 Norton parishioners.[10] However after the Act disestablishing the Welsh Church was passed in 1914, in a vote as to whether Norton parish should remain in the Hereford diocese or transfer to the diocese of St David's, the majority in the parish opted for the latter alternative and in 1920 Norton, like Knighton and unlike Presteigne, joined the diocese of St David's.

Another issue causing friction was that of the village water supply – the outlying farms were not involved as their water was supplied by gravitation or from springs. The village supply came from springs near the Hazels owned by Major Careless and in 1923 he indicated that he wished to sell the supply to Knighton Rural District Council and this heralded more than two decades of negotiations as the water pipes carrying the water was old and faulty. Knighton RDC finally took over the water supply in September 1945.[11]

Social life in Norton

The paternalistic approach of the 19th century continued for much of the first half of the 20th. According to some in the village, Powlett Milbank provided the reading room attached to one of the cottages in The Square at the junction of the Mynd and Knighton roads. When the school in The Terrace seemed likely to be too small for the growing number of children in the parish and its environs it was again Powlett Milbank who gave the site on School Lane for the new school and school house which were completed in 1908.[12]

The old school in The Terrace however did not revert to private use but continued in communal use as the Parish Room. On Sunday mornings it was used by the Sunday School, and on two or three nights a week in the winter it was the venue for the Men's Club where the members played billiards, quoits, cards and darts under the benevolent gaze of the Reverend Green Price.[13] This provided a valuable opportunity for the men, many of whom led rather solitary lives on isolated farms, to meet and socialise. In his contribution to *Memories of Norton*, Eddie Taylor also mentions the young men meeting at the church porch on Sunday evenings in the winter months to sing hymns, ballads and popular songs. This was an old custom in many parts of Wales, dating back to at least the 18th century, which had survived in Norton into the 20th.

The Parish Room was also the normal venue for the meetings of Norton Women's Institute after its formation in 1921. Though sometimes dismissed as 'Jam and Jerusalem', the WI was the first secular organisation to cater for the social needs of women in isolated communities, and gave them an informal political voice during the inter-war years on such matters as rural amenities which local councils could not then ignore. The WI also gave its members the opportunity to learn a variety of skills in such crafts as upholstery, needlework, and basket-making.[14] The Parish Room and sometimes the school was the venue for concerts, dances and whist drives, an increasingly popular pastime in the 1930s and 1940s.

In the later 1930s and the 1940s Major and Mrs Busfeild played a prominent role in the social life of the community. Each year they hosted the Sunday School Christmas party at Boultibrooke House, providing not only a magnificent tea but also a magic lantern show. By the early 1940s Mrs Busfeild had become president of the WI and most years held a garden party and sometimes a sale at Boultibrooke to raise funds for a good cause such as the local Nursing Association, which organised the district nursing service in Presteigne and Norton.[15]

Norton and the two World Wars

The Great War of 1914-18 seems to have made little impact upon Norton, possibly since only two men from the parish lost their lives in the conflict. However in March 1917, with the German submarine campaign causing food shortages and inflation, the parish meeting decided to give practical assistance to those women whose sons or husbands were serving in the Armed Forces by calling for volunteers to help cultivate their gardens.[16] The Minutes of the Parish Meetings give no indication of the outcome of the appeal however.

In 1919 a war memorial in the form of a drinking trough for livestock was placed close to the church gate with the inscription:

> The Great War 1914-18. This memorial is erected by the grateful village
> of Norton to commemorate the names of its faithful sons who fought and died
> for England and Liberty

Plate 16: The War Memorial. (Courtesy of Joan Parker)

The names of the fallen were not inscribed on the memorial and the use of 'England' rather than 'Britain' on a Welsh war memorial would appear to be a remarkable lapse. However recently another mystery has emerged, for it appears that the trough was provided by the Metropolitan Drinking and Cattle Trough Association, an animal welfare organisation, in 1919 rather than by the local community and was one of at least 16 such troughs in Wales provided by the Association.[17] By 1948 the memorial was in a poor state, but despite the appeal of Col Gilbert Drage DSO, who had purchased The Gables on the death of Whitmore Green Price, nothing was done until 1965. By this time the drinking trough served only as a receptacle for litter and to prevent this it was filled with concrete and decorated with a wrought iron sword. The dates 1939-45 were added, but the proposal that 'England' be replaced with 'Britain' could not be implemented since it was feared that this might cause further damage to the memorial. Subsequently a slate plaque bearing the names of the fallen in both world wars was attached to the memorial.

The Second World War made a much greater impact upon Norton since, following Dunkirk, thousands of troops were billeted at the Manor. At first they were in tented accommodation, but the tents were replaced by Nissen huts built on concrete foundations. Eventually the Manor became a base for military courses such as training drivers for Bren carriers and for battle training. Initially the latter took place in The Longwood behind the manor house, but soon ranged over the surrounding hillsides. This had tragic consequences on one occasion when, on 28 February 1943, two Presteigne boys were killed and several others wounded, two fatally, when a 3-inch mortar bomb, left on Stonewall Hill after a training exercise, exploded while they were examining it.

The troops treated their quarters at the Manor with casual negligence. Thus in 1943, after there had been three fires requiring the services of Presteigne Fire Brigade in little more than three weeks, Presteigne UDC felt constrained to warn the military authorities that a charge would be made for the brigade's services in future. Speeding military vehicles, wheeled and tracked, on occasion threatened life and property and damaged road surfaces, creating tension between the civil and military authorities.[18]

Another new feature of Norton life during the Second World War was the Home Guard. This started life in May 1940 as the LDV, the Local Defence Volunteers – the initials sometimes unkindly taken to mean 'Look, Duck and Vanish'. Officially the Norton Home Guard was Number 2 Platoon of B Company Presteigne of the 1st Radnor Battalion, under the command of Lieutenant J.A Busfeild – Major Busfeild's effective rank in the Home Guard. Number 2 Platoon consisted at most of 24 men, including four officers. The county contained two structures that were considered potential targets: the Elan Valley dams and the pipeline to Birmingham and the Central Wales railway line, in particular Knucklas viaduct, one of the most vulnerable points on the line, and their protection was the primary function of the county's Home Guard.

The strategic importance of these potential targets may have been brought home in the second half of 1940 when eastern Radnor experienced its first air raids of the war. That of 1 July on Gwernaffel may have targeted the pipeline, while that of 31 July near Llangunllo may have been directed at the pipeline or the viaduct. On 25 September six bombs fell near the junction of the Knighton to Presteigne and Whitton roads, three of them on Jenkinallis

Farm – possibly the result of a damaged enemy aircraft jettisoning bombs before heading back to base.[19]

Much time however was spent on humdrum training and exercises. Some did not take these too seriously and there were frequent reprimands for smoking on duty or being late on parade. Occasionally however a sense of duty was reinforced by local rivalry, as on a Sunday in June 1942 when the Llandrindod and Rhayader Companies of the Home Guard carried out a mock attack on Knighton which was defended by the Knighton and Presteigne Companies. The *Radnor Express* of 11 June reported that the defenders had been victorious and that several injuries were incurred, 'some of them real'.

Another feature of the war years in Norton was the arrival of children from the towns and cities, evacuated to escape air raids. Some of the evacuees arrived under a private arrangement when a friend or relative in Norton agreed to look after a city dweller's child or children. Others arrived under the official evacuation scheme, many of them from the Bootle area of Liverpool. Initially there was a measure of mutual incomprehension between the host families and their children on the one hand and the evacuees and their parents on the other, for in those days there was a greater gulf between urban and rural amenities and ways of life. However good will on both sides and the natural resilience of the children saw tensions ease and in some cases links between the hosts and the evacuated children have survived throughout the post-war decades.

The war also had a profound impact upon farming patterns in the parish for the German submarine campaign made increased domestic food production imperative. The arable acreage increased dramatically in Norton, by 85% by 1943 and in 1945 the arable acreage was still 75% above the 1939 figure, with barley and oats showing the largest increases in acreage. The permanent grass acreage fell sharply, by more than 60%, but stocking levels fell less steeply, cattle by 10% by 1943 and 14% by 1945, and sheep by 5% by 1943 and 9% by 1945.[20]

Farming in post-war Norton

The post-war crop and livestock returns for Norton suggest greater emphasis on permanent and temporary leys at the expense of cereals and rough grazing and increasing stocking levels, and this trend gathered pace in the last quarter of the century. Thus the 1985 returns showed the acreage under cereals, roots and potatoes etc had fallen by more than half compared with the returns of 1945, while rough grazing had fallen by two-thirds in the same period. Nor was it simply a matter of the quantity of grassland, for programmes of ploughing up and reseeding had greatly improved the quality of pasture. As a result stocking levels had greatly increased: in 1985 the number of cattle had increased by 65% over the 1945 figure and the number of sheep by nearly 90%.

The nature of livestock farming also changed over the last two or three decades of the century for the emphasis was now placed on the production of fat lambs for slaughter or store lambs for selling on, rather than on two-year-old ewes, and the great autumn sheep sales have become a distant memory. Nor have the old indigenous breeds – the Kerry Hill, the Radnor Forest or the Clun Forest – remained dominant for other breeds such as the Texel have been introduced to improve carcass quality. In the cattle sector, the previously dominant Hereford breed has made way for early maturing continental breeds such as the Limousin and the Charolais.

There has also been an increasing reliance upon grass silage, which largely reduced the need for growing forage crops such as oats and roots and the need for hay-making, an uncertain business at the best of times. Another feature has been the increasing reliance upon contractors for major routine tasks such as ploughing, mowing and harvesting, which has reduced farmers' capital and labour costs. Thus in 1975 the full time labour force (including farmers) on Norton farms amounted to no more than 15 men and 4 women workers, with 3 other men working on a part-time or casual basis, while 6 of the smaller holdings were worked on a part-time basis. There were 15 holdings in 1975 but ten years later consolidation had reduced the number of holdings of 5 or more acres to 11.[21]

Post-war Norton

For a couple of decades little changed in Norton: the population and the number of houses in the parish increased only slowly. In spite of Knighton RDC designating the village a Building Area, little new building took place due to a shortage of building materials, apart from four semi-detached houses built in 1950 on Mynd Road. The only major change in the village, and that generally considered for the worse, was the closure of the school in 1958, with its eight pupils transferring to Presteigne.[22]

The first major housing development came in 1969 when Knighton RDC built an estate of 22 prefabricated Reema houses, subsequently called Millbank (*sic*) after Sir Powlett Milbank, in the centre of the village and adjoining the B4355.[23] The council houses were built in accordance with strict cost restraints and excited considerable opposition at the parish meeting held in May 1969. It was considered that Knighton RDC had 'foisted on this parish 22 new houses of a design singularly out of character and grossly overcrowded as to be wholly alien to this hamlet'.

Moreover this was in sharp contrast with 'the exacting control exercised by the authorities over private building'. A petition protesting against the development was signed by 40 of the 70 ratepayers and led to one concession in that the unsightly flues on the Reema houses were replaced by standard chimney stacks.

There was an element of 'Nimbyism' in the opposition to the development for there was certainly a severe housing shortage in east Radnorshire, particularly in rural areas. However it seemed to be the first stage in what appeared to be unregulated expansion, since by 1971 outline planning approval had been given for housing developments at both ends of the village and planning permission was being sought for 200 caravans and a number of chalets at Norton Manor. The parish meeting of February 1971 felt that was no overall plan for this development and passed a resolution that

	Population	Occupied houses
1951	210	67
1961	230	65
1971	250	90
1981	345	142

Figure 29: Population and housing 1951-1981
(Source: Printed census data)

The meeting views with consternation the continuing haphazard development of Norton which threatens to destroy the whole character of this hitherto peaceful residential village.

However in 1973 planning permission was given first for Caefelin and later for Will's View, while the expansion of the caravan park at Norton Manor went ahead later. The last quarter of the century also witnessed some piecemeal development, mainly single houses, while in 1998 building began at Offa's View, for which planning permission for 50 dwellings had been gained in 1970. The population of Norton was 421 in 1991 and continued to grow in the opening decade of the 21st century, mainly as a result of the completion of the Offa's Green estate. The continued expansion of the village is viewed with misgiving by some who feel that the village will ultimately lose its character.[24]

In 1974, following the re-organisation of local government and possibly dissatisfied with the manner in which Knighton RDC had managed the development of the village, Norton opted to join with Presteigne to form the Presteigne and Norton Town Council and after 1984 in the Presteigne Community Council, electing 4 of the 13 councillors. In essence Norton became a suburb of Presteigne, and a dormitory suburb at that, since Norton children attended Presteigne or Whitton primary schools and John Beddoes School, while the working population not involved in agriculture commuted to Presteigne, Knighton or further afield. To make matters worse the village lost its shop and post office in 1996.

The increase in population and the increased demand for housing in Norton, Presteigne and Knighton over the last quarter century or so was the result of an inflow of older age groups from the conurbations, notably from the west Midlands, attracted by relatively cheaper housing and a more attractive environment, but with easy access by rail and road to their former home region. However this has occurred against the background of an out-migration of younger age groups in search of more favourable employment opportunities and as a result the proportion of the population over 60 increased sharply, to more than 32% in Presteigne and Norton in 2001.

The ageing of Norton has not been without social costs in the form of increased demands on medical and social services. However the elderly also provide a significant source of employment, since many in the over 60 age group require at least part-time assistance with domestic cleaning, gardening, property repairs, painting and decorating. They also provide a significant clientele for the 100 or so of the Presteigne workforce employed in the health and social welfare sectors, according to the 2001 census.[24] Again people in their 60s and early 70s increasingly regard themselves – and are regarded – as 'middle aged' rather than 'old' and, if retired and still socially active, provide many of the volunteers upon whom local social and community organisations such as the WI and the Village and Sports Committees depend. Norton Sports Day, held intermittently since 1970 and annually since 1995 bears witness to the village's continuing sense of community.

However by the closing decades of the century the nature of the village had changed drastically, for whereas it had been primarily a farming community, now relatively few in the village have more than the most tenuous links with farming. The more the village becomes a suburb of Presteigne, the greater is the risk to Norton's sense of community, for the priorities of town and country tend to diverge. To avoid this Norton must retain a strong sense of its own identity.

BIBLIOGRAPHY

Primary Sources: Manuscript

The Estate Office, Brampton Bryan
Harley papers, Bundles 1, 4, 58, 59, 64

Herefordshire County Record Office
HD 5/15/82 Norton churchwardens' presentment to the Articles of Enquiry, 1719
HD 7/15/275, HD 7/17/6, HD 7/19/6, HD 7/20/212, HD 7/20/314, HD 7/20, 7/20/463:
      Norton citations 1673, 1678 and 1679
Bishop's transcripts, Norton parish

The Judges Lodgings, Presteigne
Norton Parish Meeting Minute Book, 1894-1974

National Library of Wales
Norton parish register
Census data 1801-1901

Powys County Archives Office
Deeds relating to Old Impton, Norton 1536-1694
Order book of the Radnorshire Turnpike Trust
RD/BRA/1996/1-2 Harford Jones' marriage settlement
Norton tithe schedule, 1845
Norton Enclosure Award, 1868
R.C.B. Oliver's draft article on John Read
W.C. Maddox, *History of Radnorshire Civil Defence Scheme, 1935-46,* unpublished typescript

Radnorshire Society Library
W.H. Howse, MS manuscript notebooks T, W

The papers of John and Esther Roberts
 A copy of E.J.L. Cole's transcription of Richard Flower's will, 1626 (RSL)
Transcript of Rev. Richard Vaughan's letter of 1740 to the diocesan authorities (HCRO)
Summary of Norton Churchwardens' meetings and parish accounts, Books I & 2, 1769-1894
Sketch map of the possible boundary of the borough of Norton

The National Archives
Calendar Inquisition Post Mortem iv, No 35
SP 28/202 Norton parish return, 1647

CRES 49/4919, CRES 49/7662 Correspondence regarding Crown estates in the Lordship of
    Maelienydd
MAF 68 Parish crop and livestock returns 1875-1985, including those of Norton, Radnorshire

Primary Sources: Printed

Official Publications
House of Commons Papers, George III, Reports and Papers 1775-80, Volume 31, Poor Relief
House of Commons Papers, George III, Reports and Papers 1787-78, Volume 60, Poor Relief
Parliamentary Papers 1803-04, XIII
The India List and *The Indian Office List 1905*

Other Calendars and Papers
Alumni Oxienses 1500-1714
Alumni Oxienses 1715-1886
A.T. Bannister (ed), *The Register of Thomas Mylling, 1475-1492*, Hereford, 1919
Ifan ab Owen Edwards, *Catalogue of Star Chamber Proceedings Relating to Wales*, Cardiff, 1929
M.A.E. Green (ed), *Calendar of the Proceedings of the Committee for the Advance of Money*, 1888
Ieuan Gwynedd Jones and David Williams (ed), *The Religious Census of 1851. A Calendar of the
    Returns relating to Wales, Vol I*, Cardiff 1976
J.H. Parry (ed), *The Register of John Gilbert, 1374-1389*, London, 1915
J.H. Parry (ed), *The Register of John Standing, 1453-69*, London, 1910
Return of the Owners of Land, 1873

Contemporary printed sources
John Clark, *General View of the Agriculture of the County of Radnor*, 1794
Walter Davies, *General View of the Agriculture of South Wales*, 1815
Samuel Lewis, *A Topographical Dictionary of Wales*, 1833
Jonathan Williams, *A General History of the County of Radnorshire*, (1905 edition)

Newspapers
Hereford Journal, Hereford Times, Kington Gazette, Radnor Express, Radnorshire Standard

Thesis
D. Roy Ll. Adams, *The Parliamentary Representation of Radnorshire, 1536-1832*, MA thesis,
    University of Wales, 1970

Secondary Sources
Maurice Beresford, *New Towns of the Middle Ages*, Sutton, 1988
Llinos Beverley Smith, 'A View from the Ecclesiastical Courts: Mobility and Marriage in a Border
Society at the End of the Middle Ages' in *From Medieval to Modern Wales : Historical Essays in Honour
    of Kenneth O. Morgan and Ralph A. Griffiths*, Cardiff, 2004
    'Olrhain Anni Goch' in *Ysgrifau Beirniadol*, XIX, 1993
Colin J. Brett, 'The Fairs and Markets of Norton St Philip' *Transactions of the Somerset
    Archaeological and Natural History Society*, 2008
www.bodfachtrust.org.uk/history-of-bodfach-hall
E.J.L. Cole, 'Abstracts of Radnorshire Wills in the Prerogative Court of Canterbury' *TRS* 1936

'The Account of the Keeper of Radnor Castle' *TRS* 1963

'High Sheriffs of Radnorshire, *TRS* 1968, *TRS* 1971

www.cpat.org.uk/historicsettlementsurvey-Radnorshire-Norton

Elizabeth Dunn, 'Owen Glyndwr and Radnorshire', *TRS* 1963

M.A. Faraday, 'The assessment for the Fifteenth of 1293 in Radnor and the other Mortimer Lordships' ADD DETAILS?

'Mortality in the Diocese of Hereford', *TWFNC* 1977

'The Radnorshire Hearth Tax Returns of 1670' *TRS* 1989

Radnorshire Taxes in the Reign of Henry VIII, 2013

R.W.D. Fenn, 'Sir Richard Green Price of Norton Manor, 1803-1887', *TRS* 1985

R.W.D. Fenn and N.T. Roberts (ed), 'The *Recollections* of Laura Meredith', *TRS* 1985

J.P. Ferris, 'An Agricultural Improvement at Trewern', *TRS* 1972

www.historyofparliament/Research(Members)1558-1603

Charles Hopkinson and Martin Speight, *The Mortimers, Lords of the March*, Logaston, 2002

W.H. Howse, *Norton, Radnorshire*, 1952

'The Court Rolls of Norton', *TRS* 1964

Richard Moore-Colyer, *Roads and Trackways of Wales*, Ashbourne, 2001

www.neighbourhoodstatistics.gov.uk

Frank Noble, 'Further Excavations at Bleddfa Church' *TRS* 1964

Norton Women's Institute, *Memories of Norton*, 2001

R.C.B. Oliver, 'The Hartstonges and Radnorshire', Part I *TRS* 1973, Part II *TRS* 1974

G. Dyfnallt Owen, *Wales in the Reign of James I*, The Boydell Press, 1988

Presteigne Parish Magazine, June 1870,

Keith Parker, 'The Great Rebuilding', *TRS* 1980

A History of Presteigne, Logaston, 1997

Radnorshire From Civil War to Restoration, Logaston, 2000

'Parliamentary Enclosure in Radnorshire', *TRS* 2003

Parties, Polls and Riots, Logaston, 2009

The Story of Knighton, Logaston, 2012

www.powysenc.weebly.com//llanfrynach

Paul Remfry, *The Castles of Radnorshire*, Logaston, 1996

Royal Commission on Ancient Monuments in Wales and Monmouthshire, *Inventory of the Ancient Monuments in the County of Radnorshire*, 1913

Richard Suggett, *Houses and History in the March of Wales: Radnorshire, 1400-1800*

Dorothy Sylvester, 'Glasbury, Norton and the Problem of the Nucleated Village in Radnorshire', *TRS* 1967

The Rural Landscape of the Welsh Borderland, 1969

J.B. Sinclair and R.W.D. Fenn, *The Facility of Locomotion, Kington*, 1991

www.tudorplace.com/Documents/aldermen-of-London

www.tudorplace.com/Documents/mayors-and-sheriffs-of-London

M.E. Yapp, 'The Establishment of the East India Company in Baghdad 1795-1806', *SOAS Bulletin*, 30, 1967

The Strategies of British India: Britain, Iran and Afghanistan, Oxford, 1980

REFERENCES

Abbreviations

CPAT	Clwyd Powys Archaeological Trust
HCRO	Herefordshire County Record Office
HJ	*Hereford Journal*
HT	*Hereford Times*
KG	*Kington Gazette*
PCAO	Powys County Archives Office
RCAM	Royal Commission on Ancient Monuments in Wales and Monmouthshire
RE	*Radnor Express*
RS	*Radnorshire Standard*
RSL	Radnorshire Society Library
SOAS	School of Oriental and African Studies
TNA	The National Archives
TRS	*Transactions of the Radnorshire Society*
TWFNC	*Transactions of the Woolhope Field Naturalists Club*

Chapter 1

1. www.cpat.org.uk/historicsettlementsurvey-Radnorshire-Norton; Maurice Beresford, *New Towns of the Middle Ages*
2. *TRS* 1957, pp.64, 68; Dorothy Sylvester, 'Glasbury, Norton and the Problem of the Nucleated Villages in Radnorshire', *TRS* 1967, p.24
3. RCAM, *Inventory of Ancient Monuments in Radnorshire*, p.132; Paul Remfry, *Castles of Radnorshire,* pp.112-113, 115
4. Keith Parker, *A History of Presteigne*, pp.11-12
5. R.T. Bannister (ed), *The Register of Thomas Mylling, 1472-92*, p.67; P.E. Hair, 'Chaplains, Chantries and Chapels of North West Herefordshire *c*.1400, Part II', *TWFNC* 1989, p.272
6. J.H. Parry (ed), *The Register of John Gilbert, 1374-89*, p.58; J.H. Parry (ed), *The Register of John Standing, 1453-69*, pp.182, 184-85; R.T. Bannister (ed), *The Register of Thomas Mylling, 1475-92*, p.107
7. This section is based on *Castles of Radnorshire* and Charles Hopkinson and Martin Speight, *The Mortimers*
8. M.A. Faraday, 'The Assessment for the Fifteenth of 1293 in Radnor and the other Mortimer Lordships, Part I', *TRS* 1973
9. TNA, *Calendar Inquisition Post Mortem*, iv, No 235
10. *The Mortimers*, p.151
11. *Archaeologia Cambrensis*, 1981, p.151; E.J.L. Cole, 'The Account of the Keeper of Radnor Castle', *TRS* 1963, p.37. I am indebted to Geoffrey Ridyard for these references.
12. Frank Noble, 'Further Excavations at Bleddfa Church', *TRS* 1967, pp.60-61; *Castles of Radnorshire,* pp.63-64, Elizabeth Dunn, 'Owen Glyndwr and Radnorshire', *TRS* 1967, pp.32-33
13. M.A. Faraday, 'Mortality in the Diocese of Hereford', *TWFNC* 1977, pp.165-68

Chapter 2

1. Richard Suggett, *Houses and History in the March of Wales Radnorshire 1400-1800*, p.140
2. M.A. Faraday, *Radnorshire Taxes in the Reign of Henry VIII*, p.22; Keith Parker, *Radnorshire from Civil War to Restoration*, p.16
3. Llinos Beverley Smith, 'A View from the Ecclesiastical Courts: Mobility and Marriage in a Border Society at the end of the Middle Ages' in *From Medieval to Modern Wales*, and 'Olrhain Anni Goch' in *Ysgrifau Beirniadol* xix
4. Dorothy Sylvester, *The Rural Landscape of the Welsh Borderland*, p.503
5. *Radnorshire Taxes*, p.22; E.J.L. Cole, 'Early High Sheriffs of Radnorshire', *TRS* 1968, p.52, *TRS* 1971, p.69
6. *Radnorshire Taxes*, p.22; PCAO 'Deeds relating to Old Impton 1536-1694', Deeds 6 and 10
7. Colin J Brett, 'The Fairs and Markets of Norton St Philip', *Transactions of the Somerset Archaeological and Natural History Society*, 2008
8. PCAO 'Deeds relating to Old Impton', Deeds 15,16,18
9. www.tudorplace.com/Documents/aldermen-of-London; www.tudorplace.com/Documents/mayorsandsheriffs-of-London; TNA PRO CRES 49/4913
10. W.H. Howse, *Norton, Radnorshire* and E.J.L. Cole, 'Abstracts of Radnorshire Wills in the Prerogative Court of Canterbury, *TRS* 1936, p.11
11. www.historyofparliament/Research)Members)1558-1603; Harley papers at Brampton Bryan, Bundle 58; PCAO W.H. Howse MS notebook T, p.175

Chapter 3

1. *A History of Presteigne*, pp.54-5
2. G. Dyfnallt Owen, *Wales in the Reign of James I*, pp.164-65; Ifan ab Owen Edwards, *A Catalogue of Star Chamber Proceedings relating to Wales*, p.216; Harley Papers at Brampton Bryan, Bundle 64
3. PCAO, R,C.B. Oliver's draft article on John Read
4. R.C.B. Oliver, 'The Hartstonges and Radnorshire, Part II', *TRS* 1974, pp.26-28
5. R.C.B. Oliver, 'The Hartstonges and Radnorshire, Part II', *TRS* 1974, p.28
6. *Houses and History in the March of Wales*, p.10
7. Harley Papers at Brampton Bryan, Bundle 4
8. Harley Papers at Brampton Bryan, Bundle 58
9. RSL, W.H. Howse, MS notebook p.53; Keith Parker, *The Story of Knighton*, pp.29-30'; *Calendar of the Committee for the Advance of Money*, p.1123, TNA PRO SP19, pp.24-25
10. Harley Papers at Brampton Bryan, Bundle 58
11. Harley papers at Brampton Bryan, Bundle 58
12. This account of the administration and the customs of the manor of Norton is based on W.H. Howse, 'The Court Rolls of Norton', TRS 1964, pp.48-51
13. Dorothy Sylvester, 'Glasbury, Norton and the Problem of the Nucleated Village in Radnorshire', *TRS* 1967, pp.24-26
14. R.W.D. Fenn, 'Sir Richard Green Price of Norton Manor, 1803-1887', *TRS* 1985, p.59
15. TNA PRO SP 28,202, Norton parish return, 1647
16. Keith Parker, *Radnorshire from Civil War to Restoration*, p.165
17. HCRO HD 7/15/275, HD 7/19/6, HD 7/19/309, HD 7/20/212, HD 7/20/304
18. M.A. Faraday, 'The Radnorshire Hearth Tax Return of 1670, Part I', *TRS* 1989, pp.33-36
19. D. Roy Ll Adams, *The Parliamentary Representation of Radnorshire, 1536-1832*, University of Wales MA thesis, 1970, p.18. Footnote 1
20. 4th part of the Second Schedule, Norton Tithe schedule, 1845

Chapter 4
1. Harley Papers at Brampton Bryan, Bundle 1
2. www.bodfachtrust.org.uk/history-of-bodfach-hall
3. www.powysenc.weebly.com//llanfrynach
4. *HJ* 16.3.1796, 7.6.1797
5. W.H. Howse, 'The Court Rolls of Norton', *TRS* 1944, p.50
6. Harley Papers at Brampton Bryan, Bundle 59
7. *A History of Presteigne*, p.101; *The Story of Knighton*, p.40
8. *Alumni Oxienses 1500-1714*; *Alumni Oxienses 1715-1886*
9. HCRO HD 5/15/92
10. The papers of John and Esther Roberts: a letter from the Revd. Richard Vaughan to the Hereford diocesan authorities, 1740
11. The papers of John and Esther Roberts: Norton churchwardens' meetings and parochial accounts, Volume I
12. *House of Commons Papers, George III, Reports and Papers 1775-1780, Vol 31, Poor Relief, 1776 Returns; House of Commons Papers, George III, Reports and Papers, 1787-88, Vol 60, Poor Relief*
13. Norton churchwarden's meetings and parochial accounts, 1785
14. PCAO, R/QS/S/399 Order Book of the Radnorshire Turnpike Trust

Chapter 5
1. *Return of the Owners of Land, 1873*, Radnorshire and Herefordshire
2. J. Clark, *General View of the Agriculture of the County of Radnor, p.22*; Walter Davies, *General View of the Agriculture ....of South Wales, Vol II*, p.288
3. *Parliamentary Papers 1803-04*, xiii, An Abstract of Answers and Returns relative to the Expense and Maintenance of the Poor, pp.708-11
4. *HJ* 14.9.1814
5. *HJ* 21.9.1814, 20.10.1815, 7.1816, 28.2.1816, 24.12.1817, 27.3.1822
6. Norton churchwarden's meetings and parochial accounts
7. PCAO Norton Tithe Schedule and Map, 1845
8. The account of the restoration of the parish church is based on HT 12.9.1868 and 19.9.1868 and R.W.D. Fenn, 'Sir Richard Green Price of Norton Manor, 1803-87, TRS 1985, pp.57-60
9. 'The *Recollections* of Laura Meredith' *TRS* 1985
10. Ieuan Gwynedd Jones and David Williams, *The Religious Census of 1851. Calendar of Returns relating to Wales, Volume I*, p.681
11. *HT* 28.3.1863, 14.9.1867
12. PCAO Norton Enclosure Award
13. *HJ* 14.9.1814, 25.6.1817
14. TNA MAF 68 parish crop and livestock returns. The percentages cited refer to 3 year mid-decennial averages. Dorothy Sylvester, *TRS* 1967, p.25
15. *HT* 29.4.1882

Chapter 6
1. RSL W.H. Howse, MS notebook T, p.176; *HJ* 30.9.1829
2. *The Parliamentary Representation of Radnorshire*, p.490, *RE*, 12.5.1904
3. Recollections, *TRS* 1985, pp.72-74
4. *Keith Parker,* Parties, Polls and Riots, p.21; *The Story of Knighton*, pp.63-65, 70-77
5. 'Sir Richard Green Price of Norton Manor', *TRS* 1985, p.57
6. 'Sir Richard Green Price of Norton Manor', *TRS* 1985, p.60

7. Recollections, *TRS* 1985, pp.74, 76-77
8. Recollections, *TRS* 1985, pp.73, 76-77, 80, 82-83
9. *HT* 4.11.1865, 13.1.1872
10. *HT* 14.3.1863, 21.3.1863
11. Keith Parker, 'Parliamentary Enclosure in Radnorshire', *TRS* 2003, p.137
12. J.B. Sinclair and R.W.D. Fenn, *The Facility of Locomotion*, pp.68-69
13. *Parties, Polls and Riots*, p.53; *HT* 4.5.1899
14. 'Sir Richard Green Price of Norton Manor' *TRS* 1985, pp.60-61; *HJ* 3.7.1886
15. 'Sir Richard Green Price of Norton manor, *TRS* 1985, pp.63-64

Chapter 7
1. Jonathan Williams, *History of Radnorshire*, p.400; J.P Ferris, 'An Agricultural Improvement at Trewern', *TRS* 1972, pp.23-24; R.C.B. Oliver, 'The Hartstonges and Radnorshire, Part I', *TRS* 1973, p.43; PCAO R/D/BRA/1996/1-2, Harford Jones' marriage settlement
2. *The Parliamentary Representation of Radnorshire*, p.430; M.E. Yapp, *Strategies of British India*, pp.62-63
3. Samuel Lewis, *A Topographical Dictionary of Wales, Vol II*, p.317
4. Keith Parker, 'The Great Rebuilding', *TRS* 1980, pp.22-26
5. TNA 49/4919-20 and 49/7882 Lordship of Maelienydd Correspondence
6. M.E. Yapp, 'The Establishment of the East India Company in Baghdad, 1795-1806', *SOAS Bulletin* 30 (1967), p.336; *Strategies of British India*, p.59
7. *Parliamentary Representation of Radnorshire*, pp.452-57
8. *Parliamentary Representation of Radnorshire*, pp.445-48
9. *HT* 20.10.1857; The Moberly descent from Peter the Great of Russia has been kindly provided by Bennett family historians.
10. *HT* 30.10.1857
11. *HT* 31.12.1853; *HJ* 28.12.1853, 11.1.1860
12. *HT* 5.8.1854, 20.6.1891; *HJ* 12.3.1864
13. *A History of Presteigne*, pp.156-57; *Presteigne Parish Magazine*, June 1870
14. *HT* 12.7.1862
15. *HT* 13.8.1864
16. *HT* 21.5.1864; HJ 12.12 1865, 3.11.1866; *KG* 23.6.1874
17. *HJ* 4.9.1861, 16.7.1864, 23.7.1864, 29.6.1872
18. *HT* 26.1.1895; *RE* 27.10.1898, 11.10.1900, 17.10.1901, 18.9.1902
19. *RE* 9.7.1903, 16.6.1904
20. *RE* 11.4.1901

Chapter 8
1. *HT* 4.8.1900
2. *RE* 4.9.1919
3. *RE* 22.3.1923, 9.8.1923, 27.9.1923
4. TNA PRO MAF 68, Norton parish crop and livestock returns for 1895 and 1985
5. *HT* 29.7.1920, 5.8.1920, 16.9 1926, 16.9.1931
6. MAF 68 Norton parish crop and livestock returns, 1935,1945
7. Parish Meeting Minutes, 4.12.1894, 28.3.1896, 6.3.1939
8. Parish Meeting Minutes, 17.9.1909, 18.8.1919, 30.3.1925
9. *India List and Indian Office List, 1905*; for JA Busfeild see www.thepeerage.com; Parish Meeting Minutes 31.5.1937, 13.8.1940

10. *RS* 13.7.1912
11. Parish Meeting Minutes, 11.6.1923, 13.8.1924, 8.12.1943, 11.3.1946
12. Parish Meeting Minutes, 18.9.1905
13. *Memories of Norton*: Mrs Hester Powell
14. *Memories of Norton*: Miss Edith Wilding
15. *Memories of Norton*: Mr Eddie Taylor; Miss Edith Wilding
16. Parish Meeting Minutes, 29.3.1917
17. Personal correspondence with Mr Alan Underwood
18. *Memories of Norton*: Mr Mike Edwards; *A History of Presteigne*, p.210
19. PCAO, W.C. Maddox, *History of the Radnorshire Civil Defence Scheme, 1935-46*, unpublished typescript, p.4
20. MAF 68 Norton parish crop and livestock returns 1939,1943, 1945
21. MAF 68 Norton crop and livestock returns 1975
22. Parish Meeting Minutes, 15.5.1957, 6.1.1958
23. The account of the expansion of the village is based on Parish Meeting Minutes from 8.5.1969 to 16.8.1973
24. www.neighbourhoodstatistics.gov.uk

INDEX

Several entries are grouped under agriculture or Norton

Walking the Old Ways of Radnorshire:
the history in the landscape explored through 26 circular walks
by Andy and Karen Johnson

The walks explore Radnorshire's past, with each walk passing or visiting features about which some background information is given. These include churches, nonconformist chapels, castle sites, dykes, tumuli and other prehistoric remains, Roman forts, a battlefield, medieval houses, spas, upland farming systems, drovers' roads, squatter settlements, inns and a dismantled railway line. Several sites can only be reached on foot. Some walks follow river valleys whilst many more wander Radnorshire's rolling hills and provide expansive views. Others explore its towns and their nearby landscape. The walks range from 3½ to 10½ miles in length, with the majority being between 4 and 7½ miles. Each walk has a sketch map and detailed directions, together with background information about features en route.

Paperback (with flaps), 208 pages, over 200 colour photographs and 27 maps   Price £12.95

Walking the Old Ways of Herefordshire:
the history in the landscape explored through 52 circular walks
by Andy and Karen Johnson

Each walk passes or visits a number of features about which some background information is given. These include churches, castle sites, deserted medieval villages, landscaping activity, quarrying, battle sites, dovecotes, hillforts, Iron Age farmsteads, Saxon dykes and ditches, individual farms and buildings, squatter settlements, almshouses, sculpture, burial sites, canals, disused railway lines – to name but a few, and including some that can only be reached on foot. The walks have also been chosen to help you explore Herefordshire from south to north, west to east, from quiet river valleys to airy hilltops, from ancient woodland to meadows and fields, from remote moorland to the historic streets of the county's towns, and of course Hereford itself. The walks range from 2½ to 9½ miles in length.

Paperback (with flaps), 384 pages, over 450 colour photographs and 53 maps   Price £12.95

The Drovers' Roads of the Middle Marches
their history and how to find them today, including sixteen circular walks
by Wayne Smith

This is the story of the men who until as recently as the 1930s used to walk with their sheep and cattle out of Wales along the ancient trackways to the markets and fairs of England. The journeys were carefully judged – too slow and the expenses of feeding and accommodating men and beasts would mount, too fast and the animals would lose condition. Droving was a steady trade, and the drovers were often entrusted with commissions and even money to be taken to London, a practice from which the first banks developed. Tell-tale signs of droving routes can still be discerned in the landscape. Wayne Smith describes the routes the drovers took, and includes sections in 16 circular walks, all illustrated with his own photographs.

Paperback (with flaps), 176 pages, 50 colour and 12 b/w photos, 17 maps   Price £10

Shadows in the Hay
Landscape, nature and the passage of time on a Herefordshire farm
by Colin Williams

The discovery of a batch of old photographs of a farm in Herefordshire that once belonged to his great-grandfather, and a conversation with his grandmother about her memories of life on the farm, inspired nature writer Colin Williams to go there on foot and walk the land his ancestors once tended. The journey prompted reflections: what is it about our relationship with where we live that gives us our understanding of 'home', and how has that changed over the generations since the days when his family worked the land of Wolf Point?

Hardback, 144 pages, with 40 b/w photos   Price £12.95

The Archaeology of Herefordshire: An Exploration
by Keith Ray

Keith Ray was Herefordshire's County Archaeologist between 1998 and 2014, during which time he generated a wide range of exploratory projects, including many excavations. Much new knowledge and understanding of Herefordshire's archaeology has been gained as a result. In this study, he has described what is now known of the county's archaeology, assessing both the work of past generations and the discoveries of this modern era of enquiry. New insights are gained on the activities and rituals of our Neolithic ancestors, the ebb and flow of beliefs at the transition of the Neolithic into the Bronze Age, the shape of Saxon Hereford, the extent of an iron-working industry showing that Herefordshire was once a surprisingly industrial county, and much besides.

Paperback, 448 pages with 230 colour illustrations   Price £15

On the Trail of the Mortimers
With a Quiz and an I-Spy competition
by Philip Hume

This book both gives a history of the Mortimers (notably in their actions and impact on the central Marches) and includes a tour that explores the surviving physical remains that relate to the family. Partly through the good fortune of having an unbroken male succession for over 350 years, and also through conquest, marriage and royal favour, the Mortimers amassed a great empire of estates in England, Wales and Ireland; played key roles in the changing balance of power between the monarchy and nobles; deposed a king and virtually ruled the kingdom for three years; became, in later generations, close heirs to the throne through marriage; and seized the throne through battle when a Mortimer grandson became King Edward IV. A Quiz and an I-Spy have been designed to give pleasure to families wishing to find out more, with the successful completion of the latter leading to a certificate issued by the Mortimer History Society.

Paperback, 144 pages with over 75 colour photographs, maps and family trees   Price £7.50

Also from Logaston Press   www.logastonpress.co.uk

The Pubs of Radnorshire
by Tony Hobbs

This books deals with all the pubs that have existed in Radnorshire about which there is some information. There are tales of the unexpected, and not just of ghosts though these appear plentiful in Radnorshire's pubs. There is the wayward lioness that temporarily cured one guest's rheumatism; the pub described as the scruffiest in Britain; the two pints that cost £350 apiece; the mynah bird that squawked 'Whoa there' to passing horses and then ordered a drink for the bemused rider; duelling; cock-fighting; visiting royalty and celebrities ...

Paperback, 368 pages, over 450 b/w illustrations   Price NOW £6.50

Parties, Polls and Riots: Politics in nineteenth-century Radnorshire
by Keith Parker

The imposition of additional costs on Radnorshire's many small farmers in the form of tolls came on top of other grievances — declining farm incomes, tithes, high poor rates and increased local taxation — and the tollgates became an easy focus on which anger could be vented. The issues of commons encroachment and fishing rights saw more of a class divide.

Paperback, 192 pages with 40 b/w illustrations   Price NOW £4.95

The Story of Hereford
Edited by Andy Johnson & Ron Shoesmith

This book tells the story of Hereford in breadth and depth, and includes the results of recent research and archaeological investigation. Alongside more familiar aspects of the city's history – how it fared in the Civil War, the foundation and history of the cathedral, the navigation of the Wye – there is new material on Saxon Hereford, medieval trade, Georgian Hereford and the activities of freehold land societies in the Victorian period. There is also information on less well known aspects of the city's past, including Hereford's prominence as a great centre of scientific and other learning at the end of the 12th century, and the use of the city as a base by Simon de Montfort, and also by Prince Henry in the wars with Owain Glyn Dwr. Whether you are familiar with Hereford's history or completely new to it, there is much here to interest, intrigue and surprise.

Paperback, 336 pages with over 160 colour and 50 mono illustrations   Price £15